Pursuing *Your*
Passions!

How to Create a Truly Meaningful Life

Pursuing *Your* Passions!

How to Create a Truly Meaningful Life

DAVE ROMEO

iUniverse, Inc.
Bloomington

Pursuing Your Passions!
How to Create a Truly Meaningful Life

Edited by Cathy Johnson
Front Cover Photo of Tori Klabunde by Nick Willett
Front Cover Photo of Salvatore Romeo by Jasmine Grimm
Back Cover Photo by Dwight Lewis

iUniverse books may be ordered through booksellers or by contacting:

iUniverse
1663 Liberty Drive
Bloomington, IN 47403
www.iuniverse.com
1-800-Authors (1-800-288-4677)

ISBN: 978-1-4759-3980-4 (sc)
ISBN: 978-1-4759-3981-1 (e)

Printed in the United States of America

iUniverse rev. date: 7/25/2012

About the Author

Dave Romeo was born in Brooklyn, New York and grew up on Long Island. In 1984, he established a Guinness World Record for the most fish caught in a season by catching 3,001 largemouth bass in 77 days of fishing. This achievement became a pivotal point in his life as it opened up a floodgate of opportunities.

Among these opportunities were Dave's first two books entitled: *Better Bass Fishing – The Dave Romeo Way* (Sterling Publishing) in 1988 and *Dave Romeo's Long Island Freshwater Fishing Guide* (Dave Romeo Publishing) in 1990.

Dave designed a series of bass fishing lures for Panther Martin Lures and starred in a full-length instructional bass fishing video. For ten years, he ran Dave Romeo Bass Tournaments. Eventually, he decided to use what he learned from fishing and from running his own business to aid other business people.

In 1990, Dave fell in love with Kim Trout, a Lancaster County native, and moved to Lancaster County, Pennsylvania, where they married. The couple now resides in Elizabethtown, Pennsylvania.

Dave became a staffing recruiter for the printing industry in 1992. Six years later, he became an owner of

Primary Staffing Services in Lancaster, Pennsylvania. He is in charge of the Primary Seminars & Coaching by Dave Romeo division, serving as a personal and professional results coach and a national motivational speaker, primarily in the areas of sales, leadership, and personal growth. Some of his greatest influences are John Maxwell, Ken Blanchard, Dale Carnegie, Don Hutson, Harvey Mackay, Tom Peters, Anthony Robbins, Lance Secretan, and Brian Tracy. Not only has Dave read virtually every book written by these authors, but their influence can be felt in this book.

In 2000, Dave published his landmark book, *Nice Guys Finish First!* – *How to Be a Winner Without Losing Your Integrity* (Primary Publishing) establishing him as a powerful storyteller with a gift for inspiring readers.

Dave published his best-seller, *Designing Your Destiny* – *22 Steps to a Compelling Future* (iUniverse Publishing) in 2003, which has become a field-manual for people who wish to improve their lives. It has also been published in Chinese. *Designing Your Destiny* is also one of 68 electrifying seminars presented by Dave Romeo.

In 2006, Dave published *Stumbling Onto Success* – *Turning Mistakes Into Masterpieces* (Executive Books). This book maps out many strategies that have made his seminars a phenomenal success. *Stumbling Onto Success* delves deeply into the practice of goal setting (an area the author has mastered), thus making this book a worldwide sensation.

One year later, in 2007, Dave achieved another fishing milestone. He caught, recorded, and released more than 25,000 bass in 25 years. This story became the basis for the book, *Striving for Significance* (iUniverse) in 2009.

Dave also published his first spiritual growth book in 2007 entitled *Birth of a Chapel* (Dave Romeo Publishing). In 2011, Dave published his second spiritual growth book entitled *Rebirth of a Chapel* (Dave Romeo Publishing). He also published *Bass Fishing with Panther Martin Lures* (Dave Romeo Publishing) on the very same day.

This tenth book, *Pursuing Your Passions,* picks up where *Striving for Significance* leaves off, and is designed to be the second in a three-book series (joined together by the personal growth theme, the use of song titles as some of the chapter titles, and the artistic floral image of *'The Romeo Hill'* featured on the spine of these books).

Dedication

First, to my Lord and Savior, Jesus Christ. I ask You to bless this work and its readers who seek to better understand their earthly purpose.

Second, to my wonderful wife, partner, and best friend Kim. You have created clarity out of chaos. I thank you for making me come alive through your love and for igniting my spark. I look at you and I see my heart. I have learned more about love by knowing you than from any other human being. You have put meaning in my life and for that I am eternally grateful.

Third, to my father, Salvatore Romeo who entered heaven on August 13, 2010. I have heard it said that mothers raise boys, but fathers raise sons. I am so proud and honored to be your son. I ask our Father in heaven to watch over my father in heaven.

Acknowledgements

To my family, especially my incredible mother, Rita Romeo, my wonderful brother, Jack, and the rest of the Romeo, Trout, Caldeira, and Iskric clans. I love you all. Thanks for putting up with me.

I extend my appreciation to all of the members of Saint Michael the Archangel Roman Catholic Church in Windsor, PA and in particular, the Bradley, Fonticoba, Hiatt, Kearney, Kisielnicki, Mackin, Noel, Spencer, and Trott families who have become such an endless source of inspiration. I am humbled to be in your company and I strive to be in your class.

Deepest thanks to the numerous *'knowledge sponges'* who attend my seminars with insatiable enthusiasm, including Jacques and Rebekah Abreu, Stephanie Aponte (*my customer service super hero*), Siti Bahaman, Sharon Beiler, Matthew Best, Elaine Bledsoe, Chris Bookwalter, Kim Brenner-Zirkle, Hadley Brown, Scott Brubaker, Nate Bunty, Nick Carter, Melanie Clement, Mark Clossey, Mike Coulson, Jeff Dombach, JoAnn Drumheller, Cheryl Feeser, Mike Ferro, Brian Fisher, Kevin Fry, Jim Gante, John Gill, Carol Glass, Georgia Goshea, Crystal Grove, Kat Gwinn, Fran Halbleib, Melynda Hasselbach (*my twin!*), Jason Hubler, Dan Irvin,

Judy Jacobs Vargas, Bob Kandratavich, Paul Kohler, Barb Kovalsky, Carol Leas, David Leedom, Lou Leyes, Dan and Melissa Lineaweaver, Bonnie Locher, Glenda Machia, Charlie Mann, Bob McRedmond, Leon Miller, Maryanne O'Neill, John Platts, Dale Power, Scott Ray, Jon Ruffner, Nancy Seibert-Tipton, Jennifer Senft, Terry Senft, Rose Shaffer, Karen Saxe, Stephen Sikking, Morrell Sipe, Dwight Smith, Dave Spangler, Ron Stare, Mike Stern, Lareca and Randy Whitfield, Erin Woods, Kimberley Woods, and Darlene Zerbe. You have allowed me the privilege to enjoy the greatest job in the world. What would I ever do without you? I love you all dearly from the bottom of my heart.

Thanks to my mentors, coaches, and colleagues, including the late great David Boehm, Bob Buerger, Laura Douglas, Myron Golden, Becky and Jim Hoffman, Don Hutson, the late Charlie 'Tremendous' Jones, Father Denis McMahon, Sharon Mitzell, Mary Scoles, Father Gabriel Tetherow, and Brian Tracy. You have guided me well in more ways than you will ever know.

My great friends and role models including Barbara and Tim Anglim, Cathy Johnson (my fantastic editor), Bruce Cooper, Mike Fenech (gone but not forgotten), Art Gardner, Bernadette Hill, Mary Hoffman, Karen Johnson, Mark Kanterman, Peter Nicholson, and Barb and Carl Wilson. Thanks for choosing to share your lives with me.

And also to Rick Conley, Amanda Dodson, and Dwight Lewis at Primary Staffing Services, who make me *appear* respectable through my association with them.

Contents

Prologue

'More potential is wasted because of the fear of success rather than the fear of loss.'
—Dave Romeo

In a conversation with Dave Romeo Seminars Hall of Famer Jody Osborne, I experienced a revelation. It has never been a secret that I enjoy being the center of attention. Chalk it up to being an only child for a good part of my life or what have you. It is just a fact. What I never realized, or verbalized, until that conversation with Jody is that what I sought was credibility. I realized that the more credibility I exude, the more my praise and recognition of others will matter.

I wish to lavish praise upon people who inspire others to greatness and by doing so—inspire you to fuel your passions. Do not fear adversity or the criticism of others. God gave you your talents for a reason. Pursue them with great gusto. I challenge you to *pursue your passions!*

A memory stirs in my mind. It was April 3, 2003. I was just getting ready to do my seminar called *Survive and Thrive In Your Own Business* at the Eden Resort in Lancaster, Pennsylvania, when I noticed John Platts walk in and sit down. John is the owner of Platts Motors—a used car dealership—and one of my customers. What surprised me was that, while he was a frequent attendee, John was not registered for that seminar.

I said to John, *'I don't have you registered for today. Would you like to stay anyway?'* He asked me what the topic was and I told him. He decided to stay. (I am thinking to myself, *'Who goes to a seminar without even knowing what the topic is?'*) So I said to him *'John, you come to my seminars and you never say a word. What do you get from them?'* He paused for a few seconds and then he said something that has stayed with me ever since. He replied, *'You stir up ideas in my head.'*

As I thought about John's reply, it seemed to me that it was the best reason to ever go to a seminar. It became a mission of mine to make sure I was continuously challenging people who come to my seminars. It must be working because John Platts has now been to thirty of my seminars, and yet, he is not even among my top 25 all-time attendees. As Walt Disney said, *'Do what you do so well that people will come to see you do it again.'* As of this writing, my top ten all-time seminar attendees have taken a combined total of 550 of my seminars, ranging from to 47 to 66 (not including repeat seminars). Walt Disney was right. I have used his advice as a barometer to know how I am doing.

Another one of my best clients, Jennifer Senft, was introducing me one time, and lost her place. She then looked down at her notes and commented, *'Oh let me see, I don't even know which seminar this is.'* At that moment I realized that what started out as a vehicle to teach people valuable skills had been transformed into something far grander—an enriching and inspiring event that people loved to keep experiencing. The actual seminars were incidental. They had become a way to express my personal passion for serving others, and my attendees sought them out as a source of inspirational nourishment.

This symbiotic relationship has been going on for the past 14 years, and I am completely in awe that people long to be part of something so enjoyable to deliver. The intent of this book is to help you unlock your passion for expressing yourself and connect in a fulfilling way with others who share your talents.

'Be the change you wish to see in the world.'
—Anonymous

Introduction: The Hourglass

'Like sands through the hourglass,
so are the days of our lives.'
—MacDonald Carey

Did you ever take a look at an hourglass and notice how it is constructed? It is basically broken down into three parts. There is the top, the narrow opening in the middle, and the bottom. Let us use the hourglass for a moment to represent your life. The bottom grains of sand represent the passage of time which have already come and gone. They are behind you—you cannot do anything about them. They represent your past where you will store your memories.

The top represents what is yet to come. It is your future; however, in real life, you cannot clearly see just how many grains of sand you have left. That part of the hourglass is not visible to us. You should always be thinking about your future and providing for it, but you do not have the luxury of seeing it before it arrives—which brings us to part three.

The narrow part of the hourglass represents your present. You will notice that the grains of sand move most quickly here. They remind us that we need to pay attention to them now, for once they pass, they will quickly become part of our past—never to be altered again.

While time will continue to flow before you for the rest of your life, I challenge you to start paying close attention to your present and making the most of your time and your opportunities because—just as with the hourglass—the grains of sand that make up the minutes of your life will race by you ever so quickly and become your past. Cherish them as they arrive, and use them to do all sorts of wondrous things today so that someday, when you reflect on your past life, you will be filled with peace and fulfillment as you contemplate the magnificent, passionate accomplishments of your life.

I share this metaphor with you because far too often I see people talking endlessly about how bad their past was and how uncertain their future looks, but I rarely find people who are making the most of each day as it comes. Make today the day you discover your passion. Find out what truly stirs your soul and then go out and set your imagination on fire—ablaze with your contributions.

'To making it count!'
—Leonardo DiCaprio
(as Jack Dawson in the movie, Titanic)

Part I:
Preparing for Passion

Chapter 1:
The Top 20

'Go and…find your smile!'
—Patricia Wettig
(Barbara Robbins in the movie, City Slickers)

'You're either climbing or sliding.' When I read that Tony Robbins quote, I always think about the Susquehanna River. If you walk out into one of the wadeable parts of the river, you can either walk up river or you can be swept down river. That is because of the swift and powerful current. It is nearly impossible to stand still in that current for any significant period of time. That is also how I feel about life and accomplishments. You either keep moving ahead and persevere, or you will lose ground and start sliding backwards. You cannot stay still for very long.

Standing still—or not progressing—is one of my greatest fears because I equate it with mediocrity. That is why I constantly want to keep working on new accomplishments. I do not want my time on earth to be wasted.

What are your best days? Can you recall them? I never wanted to look back over my life with regret. Therefore, the antidote is to fill your life with passion and great memories. That means you must take stock of your milestones.

Since I love to track information, I came up with a list of my top 20 proudest and happiest memories, so I can see that I am making some progress and using at least a portion of my time wisely.

Although I have included them in the corresponding chapters of this book, here they are (in reverse chronological order):

1. 2011 Celebrate 40 years of friendship with my two best friends

2. 2011 Saint Michael the Archangel Roman Catholic Church opens

3. 2010 The 10th Dave Romeo Seminars Hall of Fame Awards

4. 2009 Peacock bass fishing with Art Gardner in Florida

5. 2009 The Pittsburgh Penguins win the Stanley Cup

6. 2008 *The Big 5-0!* 50th Birthday Bash seminar

7. 2007 Catching and Releasing Bass # 25,000 in 25 years

8. 2005 Fishing at Loch Ness, Scotland

9. 2004 Saints Peter & Paul Roman Catholic Mission opens

10. 2002 *Designing Your Destiny* is published

11. 2000 Bora Bora at sunset on our 10th Anniversary cruise

12. 1998 My 40th Birthday Surprise Party

13. 1990 Our Wedding Day

14. 1988 Publishing my first book *Better Bass Fishing—the Dave Romeo Way*

15. 1984 Established a Guinness World Record for bass fishing

16. 1981 The Rolling Stones at JFK Stadium in Philadelphia road trip

17. 1980 The New York Islanders win their first Stanley Cup Championship

18. 1978 Battle of the Bands victory

19. 1975 Seeing Led Zeppelin live in concert for the very first time

20. 1973 Soccer All-star game MVP

What are your top 10 or 20 memories? Have you captured your passions, your highpoints? I challenge you to do so. Yours will be different but just as meaningful to you as these are to me. See your successes and relive your happiness. It is almost like looking through a kaleidoscope as you travel back to these varied and invigorating memories of your entire lifetime, juxtaposed as you put them all down next to each other on the same piece of paper.

The top 20 list is an ideal way to see how heavily your passions impact your happiest memories. As I looked over my list, it became clear that in order for you to appreciate these events, I needed to elaborate on them more thoroughly, and as you will see, I have done so throughout this book. They tend to overlap in places, so you may see a story about bass fishing that ends up in a chapter about friendship. That is how life is—just like the waters of the mighty Susquehanna, it flows directly from one place to another.

> *'If you would find yourself, you*
> *must first lose yourself.'*
> *—Lee Chamberlin*
> *(Odile Richards from Roots II: The Next Generations)*

Chapter 2:
Ignite Your Passion

'Don't die with your music still inside you.'
— Rosita Perez

Henry David Thoreau once wrote, *'The mass of men lead lives of quiet desperation, and go to the grave with the song still in them.'* What a ghastly thought! This is not what we are intended for. It is not what I want for my life and more importantly, it is not what God wants for you.

Passions speak louder than words. You are the sum of your passions. When it comes to passions, everyone is different. In my *Designing Your Destiny* seminar, I challenge people to master a personal passion. It truly astounds me that some people say they do not have any passions, or do not even understand that a passion is a calling that beckons you. It is that activity or pursuit that you long to enjoy as a way of exploring, developing, and showcasing your God-given talent. Many people have hobbies or pastimes that they enjoy, but these very descriptions pale and limit the imagination when compared with an all-out passion. It is the difference between a job and a calling. It is an intense expression that showcases what you have to offer.

Why should you even bother pursuing your passions? To borrow a phrase from the United States Army, a passion can help you *'Be all you can be'* because until you do, you will never know the greatness you are destined to achieve. You can leave an indelible mark on the world when you find those areas that make you come alive. You can inspire others to unleash their greatness by unleashing yours. You will discover your purpose and fulfill your destiny.

Passion is the ingredient that puts spice into our lives. It allows us to express our talent and put forth our best efforts, in our work, in art, in sports, in our relationships, and in our faith.

There is a rule of 10,000 hours which states that you must dedicate 10,000 hours or more to a specific skill in order to master it. That comes to between five and ten years, depending upon the amount of time in our days we dedicate to this pursuit. Larry Byrd practiced making 500 free throws every day before he went to school. Larry Byrd is in the Basketball Hall of Fame. Think about it—how many basketball players play in the NBA and never get inducted in the Hall of Fame? The answer is most of them. How many of those players made 500 free throws every day before they went to school? The answer is very few. The point is, nothing worthwhile is ever achieved without passion.

Tony Robbins said, *'There is no greatness without a passion to be great.'* I love that quote. It fuels me to find out what I might be able to do that will matter to those I serve.

While discussing this book concept with one of my mentors, Laura Douglas, we came up with two schools of thought concerning pursuing your passions: First, that we pursue a passion because we enjoy the activity in and of itself, or second, that we do so as a means to achieving an end.

The first theory—that a passion is its own reward—is Laura's contention. In other words, we pursue dancing, singing, painting, or bowling just because we enjoy these activities. I can see the merit in this point when referring to certain endeavors; however, there are a great many other pursuits where I believe the second theory is valid.

For example, a hockey player like Sidney Crosby is passionate about playing the game of hockey, but I doubt that is enough for him. I have heard it said that, *'Sidney Crosby was born to win the Stanley Cup.'* And indeed, as of this writing, he was the youngest captain to ever accomplish that feat. I cannot imagine a player with Sidney Crosby's passion for the game ever being satisfied just to play hockey without hoisting that legendary symbol over his head.

In my own case, I did not take up bass fishing just for the fun of going fishing. It was all about honing my skills, gaining a deeper comprehension of the sport, and developing greater strategic thinking. Having dedicated over 25 years to mastering the sport, and having now caught and released over 25,000 bass, I can tell you that holding a Guinness world record in this activity was a crowning achievement that has forever altered the course of my life, but once I achieved those goals, I stopped bass fishing so I could move on to other pursuits—with no regrets.

The confidence, credibility, and opportunities, generated by those accomplishments, have spilled over into every other area of my life. And one more thing—achieving the record created an awareness that I could do something that no one else has ever done. That fired my imagination with a very important burning question: *If I could do this, what else could I do that has never before been done?*

I am challenging you to ask yourself that very same question. Whether you pursue your passion because you love running marathons or because you want to one day wear a Super Bowl ring, the choice is yours. Just get in the race, start believing in yourself, and ignite your passions now.

And by the way, I admit that there are other passions I enjoy, like doing jigsaw puzzles with my wife, Kim. I hope that never ceases, because they are, in and of themselves, enjoyable activities. Each one brings its own set of challenges, and the best part of it all is seeing each one through to its completion. So, in the end, I do not believe it matters much whether you pursue your passions to achieve some final goal, or just enjoy the activity over and over again. Just pick something you love and pour yourself into it with wild abandon.

As we journey together through this very personal book, I will show you how to identify, pursue, achieve, and benefit from your passions. So, as the great Jackie Gleason used to say, '*And away we go!*'

> *'If we don't change, we don't grow.*
> *If we don't grow, we are not really living.*
> *Growth demands a temporary*
> *surrender of security'*
> *—Gail Sheehy*

Chapter 3:
Wishes versus Wants

*'Great souls have wills but feeble ones have
only wishes. We cannot wish our way to
success. We need to take action and act.'*
—*John Maxwell*

According to Patrick Morley, *'We are the sum of our decisions'*. Please do not take that statement lightly! Think about it. You are where you are right now as a result of all the decisions you have made in your life. Are you satisfied with your outcome? Why is this so important? Let me explain.

One morning, I awoke filled with enthusiasm, ready to begin the latest *Sales Academy* program. As I reviewed my E-mail from home, I was met with message after message of people canceling out on the day's program and others.

One man said he was sick, so he wondered if he should just wait another half a year and try to take it then. He was giving up before he even started!

Another was canceling an event he had scheduled eleven months ago because he had another appointment that same day. I wondered, *'Where is the commitment?'* This person had told me how he was going to make it his goal to be successful, yet congruency eludes him. This is a financial planner. Would you want a financial planner who continually breaks his word?

Now you might think that these people lack commitment but I assure you, I have spoken with them many times. They emphatically tell me they *want* to be successful. The problem is *this is not what they want, but rather what they wish.*

You can *wish* all day long but it will not get you any closer to your goals. Author Rick Page even wrote a book entitled, *Hope is Not a Strategy.*

The reason why so many of my *Sales Academy* graduates go on to become Hall of Famers is not because they took the program, but because they rose to the occasion, and although it was not easy, they persevered, and grew stronger from the experience.

Are you this way? Do you constantly say what you want, and yet procrastinate about doing what is required to achieve your goal? If so, you are not alone. So, let me show you how to avoid the number one stumbling block to unleashing your passions. If you truly yearn to be all you can be, and lead a rewarding and fulfilling life, understand clearly that there will be challenges, set-backs, and adversities between you and your goal. Guaranteed! I did not say *'might be.'* I said *'will be.'* Rest assured that this is not only the price of greatness; it is the formula for greatness. I am not saying this to discourage you, but rather to prepare you to recognize that when you face adversity, you are being tested.

One of my Hall of Fame clients, Jon Ruffner, has faced more than his share of adversities in his life, including a car accident in which he broke both of his arms, the murder of his father by a relative, losing his job six days before Christmas, and a raging fire that destroyed the third floor of his home the night before the Super Bowl.

These tragedies might certainly have thrown even the toughest person for a loop. So how did Jon face them down? He laughs when he recalls the nickname his friends bestowed upon him when he broke his arms ('*Harmless Armless*'). He used his father's death as a turning point to teach his three young sons how to deal with loss in a positive way, and he and his family learned to be resourceful while they moved into an alternate dwelling so they could restore their fired-damaged home.

After unexpectedly losing his job in December 2007, he started his own business, Ruffner Roofing, and became a successful entrepreneur in a very short period of time.

Jon also related that one of the keys to his positive attitude is his wife Lori. She is a stabilizing factor in Jon's life. I cannot help but laugh as Jon explains that when he is '*occasionally*' having a bad day, he calls his wife on the phone to vent about problem employees, slow-paying customers, or even traffic jam inconveniences. Lori patiently waits out Jon's rant and then calmly states, *'Suck it up, Cupcake.'*

Recently, Jon brought along a childhood friend of his to one of my seminars. This was someone with whom Jon had gone to school, but not kept in touch with for many years. Now Jon was helping out his friend who had experienced some hard times of his own. It was remarkable to hear how Jon's friend described him, after seeing him so many years later. *'Jon is not the boy I remember, but he is the man I knew he would become.'*

Remember that your success will not be determined by how few obstacles you encounter, but by the way in which you handle them as they arise. You will not *wish* your way to your goals, but if you pursue them with all-out commitment, you too will learn to laugh at your set-backs and succeed in spite of them. *You can change your world, if you want it badly enough.*

'Adversity does not develop character. It reveals it.'
—Anonymous

Chapter 4:
Selecting Your Passions

**'Success is where preparation
and opportunity meet.'
—Bobby Unser**

Some people need help to determine what their passions are. You may feel the same way. You might think, *I don't have any passions or if I do, I don't know what they are.* So, how do you find your passions? Have no fear—*your passions will find you!*

Growing up with a brother five years younger than me, we did not always have much in common. We were very different in almost every way. When it came to sports, naturally my age gave me a significant advantage over Jack. It did not help that he was overweight, too. However, one summer, Jack went away to a summer camp where he was put on a strict and healthy diet. He also spent a great deal of his time playing ping pong—an activity I occasionally played but not with any regularity.

When Jack returned from summer camp, our father bought a ping pong table to encourage my brother's interest. He played against my brother, and had a very hard time matching his skill level. I had not seen Jack play since he had been back. One day, he challenged me to a game of ping pong. I did not think anything of it until I saw Jack's serve. He had mastered this sport, and put so much English on his ball that I could not beat him! He returned my serves with such calculated spin and control, that he was now at a superior level to me.

This was great for Jack because I do not even think he knew just how much he could excel at a sport. Yet, his talent was there all along. It just needed to be discovered. Summer camp allowed it to surface.

My wife, Kim, will be the first to admit that her passion is not sales. Since she worked at the Pennsylvania Department of Labor for 32 years, this was not an issue. However, when it comes time to raise money for our church through our annual fundraiser, it becomes obvious what her passion is: Kim consistently out-produces every member of our congregation. I would not have expected this of Kim, but she took such great pride in making sure that she could demonstrate her talent, and make a significant contribution to our church.

My friend, Art Gardner, worked at a lumber yard for many years until he got laid off, shortly before the place closed for good. Art has one of the most admirable work ethics of anyone I know, so it did not take him long to land another job near his home, doing maintenance on city property—primarily changing locks.

Art needed to earn some extra money to make ends meet, so he also took a part-time job at Bass Pro Shops. Fortunately for Art, he had previously done some bow and arrow target practice before he began his stint at Bass Pro. Having honed this skill allowed Art the opportunity to become an archery trainer.

One of my newer clients, Chris Bookwalter, works in sales. What distinguishes Chris from just about any other ordinary salesperson is Chris' overwhelming desire to dance. He jokingly affirms, *'I don't love dance. I am dance.'* When Chris goes to a social mixer to meet new networking contacts, every one of them will remember Chris, acknowledging, *'Oh yes, the dancer.'* That is because Chris takes the opportunity to share his passion with others, and in doing so, sets himself apart from everyone else he meets in a memorable way. This is a great example of using your passions to increase people's remembrance of you. It can go a long way to enhancing your image in a positive way, and make you more successful in your work.

Your passions are within you. Allow them to come out so you can express yourself, and impress others. Pick some of your favorite positive activities, and start finding ways to work them into greater prominence in your life. *Dare to be extraordinary!*

'Live life out loud!'
—Tom Peters

Chapter 5:
Prioritizing Your Passions

'The best measure of a man's honesty isn't his income tax return. It's the zero adjust on his bathroom scale.'
—Arthur C. Clarke

Just yesterday, I went to the doctor for my annual physical (OK—it was my first in seven years). I knew a lot about the doctor because my wife, Kim, is much better about going to see him than I am. Dr. Gilhool and I were discussing just how much Kim and I enjoy watching our favorite National Hockey League team, the Pittsburgh Penguins. Dr. Gilhool said, *'Yeah, I really thought that it is amazing that Kim is into hockey so much.'* I commented, *'You should see her during the game. She is constantly correcting the announcers when they get a player's name wrong—and I don't just mean a player on the Penguins. She also knows all the players on the opposing teams!'*

Now, I love hockey, but I do not know the players as well as Kim does. That is something on which she focuses and really shines. She has made her passion for hockey a priority in her life. I prioritize my passions differently, so while I do not enjoy going to the doctor very often, I do take my health very seriously—exercising five days a week, logging 27 and one half miles a week between the treadmill and the elliptical machines, and doing 15,000 stomach crunches a week. I do want to clarify something—exercising and running are not passions of mine. I do, however, like, that in my fifties, I can finally get back down to my high school weight. I do like that three years ago, I made a commitment to lose over 60 pounds and I did it. I do like that three years later, some of my suit pants—which had to be taken in after I lost seven inches around my waist—are still a little loose on me.

As I discussed in my book *Striving for Significance,* I decided to pursue a monumental goal—to catch, record, and release over 25,000 bass in 25 years. In 2007, I achieved that goal. One thing I learned through that experience is that you must set your priorities if you want to insure your outcome. At the same time, I wanted to manage my weight, and for a while, I did. However, I soon discovered that I only had so much discipline to go around. Even though I would pack all sorts of healthy foods for my fishing trips, there were times when I would just break down and stop for Doritos, beef jerky, and Slurpees. The reason is simple: You just cannot give your all to everything. My bass-fishing and weight-loss passions were competing with each other. They were not compatible. I knew I had to prioritize my passions. I rationalized, *'I have one chance in my life to catch 25,000 bass in 25 years. This is it. Once I do it, I can go back and really concentrate on losing any weight I gain. I will make that the priority that replaces bass fishing.'* And that is exactly what I did. With my quarter of a century-long accomplishment secure, in 2010, I made it my mission to lose all those extra pounds I had packed on while I was pursuing my bass fishing goal.

Losing weight became my top priority—and not a moment too soon. When I stepped on my digital bathroom scale on January 1, 2010, I had a very rude awakening. I was the heaviest I had ever weighed in my life. If ever there was a time for me to get serious about losing weight, it was now.

I owned 16 suits but I could just barely fit into a few of them on New Year's Day. I moved all of my *'enemy suits'* (the ones that were too tight to squeeze into) to the other side of the closet in the order of the largest to the tightest. I decided to track my progress as I lost weight by seeing when I could fit into the next largest suit. Once that suit fit, I moved that *'enemy suit'* to the other side of the closet with the *'friendly suits'* I could already wear. Then I would try on the next largest suit until it also fit.

I repeated this practice until I could fit into even the smallest suit. I could see my progress, and received plenty of positive reinforcement from trying on those suits even before anyone ever said a word about my weight loss. It took about three months before all of the *'enemy suits'* were reunited on the other side of the closet.

Naturally, after losing about 40 pounds, people started commenting on how good I looked. I must admit, that was great validation for all my hard work. As you might expect, many would ask how I did it. When I told them, most thought I was crazy because it required so much time and discipline.

I left nothing to chance. One of the first things I did was make a visual representation of my weight loss. When I lost five pounds, I took a five-pound hand weight, held it in my hand, and then put it right in front of my elliptical machine to remind me that I was no longer carrying that amount of weight on my body. I did the same thing when I lost 10 pounds, and 20 pounds, and 30 pounds. After I lost 60 pounds, I could not believe how difficult it was to lift all the hand weights. *'How did I carry this weight around all the time when it was on my body?'* I reflected.

Earl Nightingale once said, *'Whatever the majority of people is doing, under any given circumstances, if you do the exact opposite, you will probably never make another mistake as long as you live.'* There is a lot of truth in that statement. Conventional wisdom says you should only weigh yourself once a week. I decided to weigh myself all day long: when I woke up, after I exercised, after I ate, after I took a bath, when I got home from work, etc.

I got to the point where I could accurately predict my weight to within a pound before I even stepped on the scale. I also learned that my weight could fluctuate as much as 20 pounds within a one-week period—something I never knew before I started tracking my weight this closely. By that time, I had achieved my weight-loss goal. It was a good thing too—I had just about run out of hand weights!

One day, I was sitting with some of my clients at lunch after a seminar. We were again discussing my weight loss when one of my clients, Anne West, stated, *'You know, you are going to have to keep doing whatever you are doing now to lose this weight if you want to keep it off.'* I really did not think that much about Anne's comment at the time, but later on her words came back to haunt me.

After I achieved my goal weight, I decided to cut back on my exercise. I did not stop completely. In fact, I was still doing a fairly intense workout routine. However, the first time I weighed myself after *'cutting back,'* my weight jumped up about eight pounds!

Two weeks later, I suffered another weight-loss setback. On August 13, 2010, my father died suddenly. He and my mother had been living in New Port Richey, Florida, so Kim and I made arrangements to fly there for the funeral and to be with my mother. While we were there, exercising was the last thing on my mind. Most of the time, we were sitting around talking, making arrangements, going through drawers, notifying relatives, looking for important documents—oh yes, *and eating!*

When I returned home and stepped on the bathroom scale, I discovered that I had gained back 31 pounds in a month! I could not believe it! I was stunned. I thought to myself, *'Anne was right! I am going to have to keep working as hard as I did to lose the weight in order to keep it off.'* As

I stated earlier, I do not enjoy exercising, but I did enjoy the way I looked and felt. So I decided to keep up that pace and make keeping the weight off a priority.

It has now been several years since I made my commitment to stay fit, and although it does require a great deal of time and exercise, I have been able to wear my altered suits in comfort.

If this is an area in which you struggle, know that you too can achieve your goal if you are passionate about your outcome and make it a priority. It will not be easy, but it will be worth it. First, as with any passion, decide why it is worthwhile. Why are you pursuing it? You have to know this before you begin, because there will be times when it will be a struggle, and other times when your plans will be interrupted.

Next, decide why *what you want* is worth giving up *what you have.* Long-term commitments almost always give way to short-term comfort unless you are truly dedicated to the outcome, and believe that your desired outcome will be worth the painful sacrifices necessary to achieve it. As Ralph Waldo Emerson said, *'For everything you gain, you lose something.'*

Understand that your weight loss will not be as immediately noticeable to others as it is to you. When you lose the first 10 to 15 pounds, it is unlikely that anyone will comment on this. Do not be discouraged! It is harder for people to observe your weight loss through your clothes, but your clothes themselves will motivate you as you feel them becoming less snug every time you wear them.

There will come a point where everyone around you starts to notice how much weight you have lost, and it will be almost like a chain reaction. For me, it was after I had lost between 35 and 40 pounds. For women, it tends to be less—about 20 to 25 pounds I am told—depending on your starting point. At first, it might seem as if one person told another and another, but in reality, they are probably noticing a thinning in your facial features, or a tightening of your body's definition.

When people comment on your weight loss, they will invariably ask you how you did it. I jokingly reply, *'It was easy, I exercised for the first half of the day so I was too tired to eat during the second half of the day!'* Even though that was an exaggeration, there were many times when it certainly did feel that way.

It was a big advantage having a treadmill, an elliptical machine, hand weights, and an exercise mat in our home. This eliminated excuses about bad weather, crowded machines, not enough time, or worrying about my appearance—any of which might have occurred, had I been doing my exercise routine in a fitness club. Mine was a completely controlled environment and an *'excuse-free'* zone.

Since I find exercise boring, I always couple my workout with something I enjoy doing—usually watching one of my favorite movies. Our family room is equipped with an extensive entertainment system and cordless headphones, which allow me to listen to a movie, a concert, or the news without waking my wife.

I encourage you to track your progress every time you exercise. It will help you to stay motivated and gain momentum on your progress. Based on everything that I learned through pursuing this passion, here are 20 simple lessons for profound weight loss:

1. Weigh yourself all day long

2. Track your progress in weight and inches

3. Make your weight loss visual (construct a pile of hand weights)

4. Keep score (save your broken and worn out exercise equipment)

5. Limit your portions on even healthy foods

6. To lose weight on your hips, twist side to side holding hand weights
   (I now do 300 sets, five times a week, but noticed an improvement even when I started with 20 sets)

7. Use a digital scale to weigh yourself (it is harder to cheat)

8. Take warm baths as often as possible (up to an hour—bring a good book)

9. Fast when you can (this can also help you spiritually)

10. Drink water *after* you weigh yourself

11. Cut out some foods (ice cream, chocolate, donuts, candy) altogether instead of just reducing foods for a set period of time

12. Drink only water for six months

13. Break your addiction to sugar (see 11)

14. Reduce how much food you are eating (you eat far more than you need)

15. Make and display a weight-loss credo (I will explain this one shortly)

16. Get rid of clothes that are too big to wear (you are not going back)

17. Officially record your weight only once a week, always around the same time

18. When you are done eating, floss immediately

19. Flush extra salt out of your body (see 10 and 12)

20. Take the time to share what you have learned with others

Through a daily (five days a week) combination of waste elimination, three miles on a treadmill, two and one half miles on an elliptical machine, 300 twists holding 10-pound hand weights, 300 leg raises, 3,000 stomach crunches, followed by a warm bath, I discovered that I could consistently lose up to 11 pounds in one day.

My weight was something that I felt was defining me to other people in a way that I did not like or want. As a coach, people expect that you should be committed to your own goals, if you expect your clients to be committed to theirs. I knew that by successfully managing my weight, my clients could see that if I committed to my goals and achieved my desired results, they had no excuse not to do the same with their goals.

One of the tools I used to remind myself of the benefits of losing weight (or *'releasing weight'* as my good friend Steve Spangenberg, would say. Steve has *'released'* over 70 pounds) was my Weight Loss Credo which reads:

Dave Romeo's Weight Loss Credo
Losing weight will help me...

1. Increase my credibility as a Results Coach

2. Improve my appearance in front of an audience

3. Look better in my clothes

4. Feel more comfortable in my suits

5. Demonstrate congruency in my words and my actions

6. Become a positive role model to others

7. Develop greater self-control and self-discipline

8. Improve my overall health

9. Boost my energy level

10. Reduce our food bill expenses

I figured, the more benefits I named, the more I would stay committed to my passion. I made two laminated copies of this credo, taped one to my treadmill, and hung the other one in my shower from the shampoo rack. Then I repeated my credo to myself whenever I worked out or showered. It became a great tool for getting leverage on myself and staying focused on my weight loss.

Why was I so passionate about weight loss? It was because I wanted to feel that I had some control over the way I looked, and if I did not like it, I could do something about it. This only happened when I made my weight loss a priority. Earl Nightingale also said, *'You get what you think about most of the time.'* If you feel stuck, or that you are not making enough significant progress in pursuing one of your passions, I challenge you to prioritize what you are most interested in achieving. When you turn up your intensity, you will be amazed at how even the most seemingly impossible goals can be achieved.

I am frequently asked, *'What kind of people do you coach?'* to which I reply, *'My best customer is someone who is dissatisfied with his or her current level of success, and is serious about doing something to improve it.'*

That was also true about me. I was dissatisfied and got serious about changing my results. You can too.

'Nothing tastes as good as thin feels.'
—Melynda Hasselbach

Chapter 6:
Don't Buy the Trophy

'Integrity can be considered as the condition of not doing what's wrong. Character can be defined as doing the right thing, for the mere reason that it is the right thing, even if that thing is difficult and unpopular. The two sewn together make honor.'
—Chris Brady

It is important to remember why we set our accomplishments and what we expect to get out of them. You do not want to lose sight of what you set out to achieve.

Years ago when I was trying to become the first person to catch, record, and release over 25,000 bass in 25 years, two women in our church congregation, approached me with a request. They said their children liked to fish. These women knew how much I loved bass fishing, and asked me if I could organize and run a freshwater family fishing field trip. (By the way, one woman had eight children. The other had nine.) How could I refuse?

But while I knew plenty of great fishing holes, I was used to fishing by myself. Often I find myself in treacherous areas; but they are places that I know like the back of my hand, and I am familiar enough with them to negotiate my way out of a given situation. However, when fishing with little children, I knew that safety had to be the primary factor. I had to find a place that had adequate parking, rest rooms, picnic tables, public access, and a strong, solid, shallow shoreline. I remembered that Little Buffalo State Park in Perry County, PA offered all of these amenities. It was a good distance away, but at least I knew everyone would be safe.

The women who asked me to run the event put big posters up in the basement of our church announcing *'Fish with Guinness World Record Holder Dave Romeo who has caught over 16,000 bass.'* I was getting concerned about all the buildup because I do my best fishing when I am alone, usually in small, familiar farm ponds. I said to my wife, *'I think I'm going to disappoint a lot of children tomorrow because I do not usually do well on big lakes, and I haven't fished there in six years.'* She said, *'I think you're making too much of this. It's not about you.'* I knew she was right.

The next day we made our trip up to the park. When everyone arrived, all the fathers were taking their little children fishing. They were having a blast and so was I! I was helping the kids bait their hooks as well as taking fish off their hooks, and the good news is that, by the end of the day, all the people who came had caught fish—with one exception. *I couldn't buy a fish!* The closest I came to taking something out of the water was when I went into the lake in my chest waders *(correction—my leaky chest waders)*, and retrieved a misdirected soccer ball with a large branch and flung it on the shore. At that point, one of the father's from the chapel told all the kids, *'Let's hear it for Mr. Romeo!'* They all yelled, *'Yeah!!!!!!!'* It felt more like they were saying, *'Hey, look, he's not completely useless!'*

I did not expect to catch much there, but I did make arrangements to fish a private pond owned by my business partner after the rest of the party left for home. When our group outing was over, we all sat together to have a noontime lunch at the nearby picnic area. I was good—I stayed and ate with the others for over an hour before finally departing.

According to the street atlas I was using, Conley Pond was several pages away from my current location so it took quite a while to reach it. But as I traveled, I noticed the atlas showed another body of water up ahead on my right. Judging by the size and location of it on the map, I expected to see a pond close enough to give it a once over.

When I located this pond, it looked ideal. The edge was lined with heavy vegetation and places where bass love to lie in wait of easy prey. There were no fences or signs. It was right along the side of the road with easy access. There were no houses on that side of the road and I did not see anyone from whom I could learn if I needed any special permission to fish there. I decided to try the pond. I thought if someone does see me, maybe they can tell me who owns the pond and I could inquire about getting permission to fish there.

I made the first cast. *Pow!* A largemouth bass. I made another cast. *Pow!* Another largemouth bass. I made a third cast. *Pow!* Bass number three! I caught six bass on six casts. Ask any angler if this is good, and they will tell you, *'yes.'* Now, couple this success with my embarrassing morning results, and you can imagine why I felt like I was on *Candid Camera*. At that point, I was very tempted to call all the fathers and say, *'I know you don't believe I know how to catch a fish, but if you could just drive up here for a few moments I can prove to you that I actually do know how to catch fish.'*—but that would have been too silly.

I continued to fish the pond until about 4:10 PM. By then, I had caught 45 bass in just over three hours. I wanted to leave enough time to get to Conley Pond which was still a little distance away. I made it to my original destination, and caught an additional 42 bass! I had now caught 87 bass since one o'clock in the afternoon. It was the single best day of fishing I had had in the past three years!

When I got back home that night, I said to my wife, *'I've got a big problem. All those boys watched me fish all morning long without catching a single bass. They know that I was going fishing after they left. They are going to ask me how I did, and I am going to look at them with a straight face and say I caught 87 bass yesterday afternoon and they will all think that I'm a liar!'*

Once again Kim said, *'I think you're making too much out of this.'* Again, I sensed she was right—and right she was. Not only did no one ask me how I did, not one of those boys even made eye contact with me!

Since I expected that I would do poorly at the freshwater family fishing day event, I decided to take the following Monday off and go fishing. My initial thought was, *'If I could catch 87 bass starting at 1:00 PM, I'll bet if I start out first thing in the morning, and fish those same ponds all day, I could catch over 100 bass in a day'*—a feat I had not previous accomplished.

I left my house early the next day and headed toward that newly-discovered pond; however when I looked at the road atlas, I found yet *another new pond!* I only caught six bass, so I decided not to invest too much time there, for fear I would miss out on the better results I anticipated at the other two ponds.

Since I was coming directly from my house, I approached the pond from the opposite direction than I had on the previous trip. With the street atlas to guide me, I kept looking for that pond—but I could not see it. I started to doubt myself, thinking, *'Did I just imagine that pond? Was it a mirage? Where is it?'*

As I drove up the rural Perry County road, I caught a glimpse of sunlight reflecting off the surface of the choppy water in my rearview mirror. *There it is!* No wonder I had missed the pond. Because I was approaching it from a different angle, I did not realize that the pond was hidden from view behind a slight rise, obscuring it until I had driven completely by it.

By the time I saw the pond, I was quite a distance past where it was located. With renewed enthusiasm for the rediscovered fishing hole, and a slight validation that I was not losing my mind, I made a U-turn so I could get back to the pond. As I attempted this maneuver (honed through many years of driving in New York), my automobile came to an immediate stop right in front of a telephone pole. On the pole was a sign that read: 'Posted: No Trespassing. No Hunting. No Fishing. *No Dave Romeo!*' (Alright—the last one was not really there *but it sure felt like it was!*)

My heart sank when I read that sign. The reason I had not noticed it two days earlier is because there were no telephone poles close to the pond, yet there was a sign on every pole on that side of the street. I drove up and down that unpopulated road, desperately hoping to find someone who could point me in the direction of the property owner, but it was all in vain. There were very few houses, and those appeared to be closed up or abandoned. There was no one around to ask, and so I had to deduct the 45 bass I had previously caught in the forbidden pond, because I did not rightfully have permission to catch them.

I made my way up to Conley Pond in hopes of salvaging some of my long trip. I only caught 16 bass there. By the way, did I mention that it rained the entire day?

Defeated, cold, and wet, I made my way back to my home base of Lancaster County, where the farm ponds are plentiful and familiar. At that point, I decided to go to some of my more reliable fishing holes. By the end of the day, I had logged about 75 miles and caught a total of 47 bass—enough to replace the 45 bass I had deducted from Saturday's catch.

The point of this long, but sadly true, fish story is *don't buy the trophy.* It is one thing to win a trophy and be recognized for accomplishing something significant. It is quite another to go out and just purchase an award which you did not earn. Yes, I was disappointed that I could not count those bass, but had I known I did not have permission to catch them, I would not have been on that land. I still achieved my goal of catching and releasing 25,000 bass in 25 years in spite of this minor setback. Yet, it is far more rewarding to know that I did so on the up and up, and that my achievement was not tainted.

I am sure that you realize that this lesson has very little to do with fishing and everything to do with character. In life, you will always find places where you might be able to get away with something you know you should not do. The question is, will you do it, or will you avoid the temptation and do the right thing?

This is the essence of pursuing your passion—it will reveal who you are to yourself, and others. People who always want a handout will not trouble themselves to work hard and earn their rewards. People who cannot be bothered with the discipline and time required for mastering a task will just pay someone else to perform it. But remember, there is a personal satisfaction that comes from doing things—especially difficult things—for yourself.

My point is that anything worth doing is worth doing with integrity, and that includes your passions. The choice is yours. Your passion will teach you more about yourself than it will about a given activity. I challenge you to put all you are into what you do as you pursue your passions, and let others learn from your example what it truly means to win with integrity.

> *'Do a job, big or small,*
> *do it well, or not at all.'*
> *—Jimmy Madonna*

Chapter 7:
One Size fits One!

*'If you don't have a plan for yourself,
you'll be part of someone else's.'*
—American proverb

Most people think of themselves as different but not necessarily unique. If someone were to describe you as 'different,' you might take it as a negative meaning. After all, you are not like anyone else. However, if someone were to describe you as 'unique,' I believe you would see that in a more positive light. That is exactly my point. All of us are unique in so many different ways. True, there are some things that you have done that many others have also done. Yet, when you look back on your accomplishments, your skills, the application of your experiences, and your interactions with other people, you will realize that there is not now, nor has there ever been, nor will there ever be, an individual quite like you. *You are completely unique.*

When I was 25 years old, I happened to fish my way into the *Guinness Book of World Records* by catching 3,001 largemouth bass in 77 days of fishing. As a result of that one accomplishment, it set off a chain reaction of countless other positive experiences in my life—one of which was starting up my own business called Dave Romeo Bass Tournaments. It was an incredible learning experience. I absorbed so much about being an entrepreneur. I ran that business for 10 years, and *owned* 100% of the freshwater bass fishing tournament market on Long Island, NY for the entire time. Later, when I became a results coach, I drew from those lessons to help teach other entrepreneurs how to successfully run their businesses.

The reason I make that point is because when I was getting started, the president of a major fishing lure company told me that if I was going to *'make it'* in the bass fishing tournament business, I was going to have to become a competitive bass angler. That meant that I would have to buy a top of the line bass boat, a boat trailer, and a truck with which to pull them. In addition, I would be driving all over the country, plunking down about $10,000 for the entrance fees in someone else's bass fishing tournaments in order to compete for national sponsors. In other words, *he was advising me to be just like everyone else.*

I had a few concerns about his advice. First, I did not have the amount of money it would have taken to follow his instructions. Second, I did not have any interest in doing what he suggested—hauling a boat behind a truck across this big country sounded like a pretty grueling experience. Third, I had no desire to be like everyone else!

I have subscribed to B.A.S.S. (Bass Anglers Sportsman Society) Magazine since I was 24 years old. Each issue contained numerous advertisements for fishing-related products from boats, to lures, to fishing rods. The first year I started reading that magazine, I noticed that the same bass tournament angler was featured in virtually every ad. It was the person who had won the most recent Bassmaster Classic—*the Super Bowl of Bass Fishing.* Ironically, the next year, a different angler won the Bassmaster Classic and, as you may have guessed, the newest winner replaced the previous winner in all the ads throughout the magazine. You hardly ever saw the previous winner in any more ads after that.

This happened again and again over the years. I thought to myself, *'Why would I want to spend all that time and money trying to be like all these other anglers when I am already the only living Guinness World Record Holder?'* Basically, I did the opposite of what that fishing tackle lure president told me I had to do if I wanted to attract national sponsors for my fishing tournaments. Despite not taking his advice, I managed to attract 16 national sponsors—virtually every one of them being the number one-rated brand in its respective category— but you can judge that for yourself.

Dave Romeo Bass Tournaments National Sponsors:

1. Eagle Claw (Wright and McGill Co.) Rods, Reels, and Hooks
2. DuPont Stren Fishing Line
3. Plano Tackle Boxes
4. Minnkota Electric Trolling Motors
5. Sea Eagle Inflatable Boats
6. Bill Lewis Lures (Rat-L-Traps)
7. Panther Martin Lures (Harrison-Hoge Industries)
8. Culprit Plastic Worms (Classic Manufacturing Co.)
9. Fisherman Eyewear Polarized Glasses
10. Humminbird Depth Finders
11. Uncle Josh Bait Company (Pork Rinds)
12. PreSun Sunscreen (Bristol Meyers)
13. Fleck Spinner Baits
14. Powerpak Spring-wound Lures
15. Gaines/Phillips Company (Bass Poppers)
16. Bass Hunter Boats

I picked up so many sponsors that I had to start turning away other companies which competed in the same product lines of my existing sponsors. Incidentally, the same fishing tackle president who told me that I would not attract national sponsors unless I competed in other national bass tournaments, owned two of the sponsoring companies listed above.

In 2002, I wanted to get my book *Designing Your Destiny* published, and from several previous conversations with people in the book-selling industry, I expected that a publisher would pay for the rights to publish it. Unfortunately, that was not the case.

At the time, self-help and personal growth books were flooding the bookstores. I was first told by one publisher that I would need to spend about $30,000 on a public relations campaign, go on *Oprah* and *The Montel Williams Show* to promote the concept and then, maybe the publisher would consider publishing my book.

I thought about having one of my many printing company clients publish the book, but that still would have cost about $9,000. My brain would not shut off. All I did was think about how I could get that book published.

Finally, I was talking with a man who had helped me flow the text on my previous book and I explained to him about the trouble I was having finding a publisher. As it turned out, this man was also in the process of having a book published. He said, *'Have you ever considered having your book published by an internet publisher?'* I asked him what he meant, and he said, *'iUniverse has an arrangement where you can submit your manuscript to them on-line, and for only $449.00 they will publish five copies of your book in 90 days.'* He added, *'You can buy as many copies of your book as you want at a reduced price, and iUniverse will print additional copies of your book on* *demand as people order it, and pay you royalties on the sales.'*

After our phone conversation, I looked up iUniverse on line, and found that, in fact, my friend was absolutely right! After three months, I was holding my teal-colored first copy of *Designing Your Destiny* in my hands. It became my bestselling book to date, and has since been published in Chinese. Not only that, but my seminar of the same name has long been my highest grossing seminar of all time. It was another reminder that if you want something badly enough, keep asking yourself, *'How can I make sure this happens?'*, and if you do not get an answer, just keep asking with total expectancy until you discover your answer.

The point is, when you pursue your passions, remember that they are indeed *your passions*—not someone else's. You had better brace yourself to be told that what you want to do will not work. That is usually because no one else has done what you long to do (or, perhaps more accurately, no one with your unique set of accomplishments, skills, experiences, and interactions with other people). So I challenge you to go do it anyway and show them how it is done.

> **'You do not merely want to be considered just the best of the best. You want to be considered the only ones who do what you do.'**
> **—Jerry Garcia**

Part II:
Pursuing Your Passions

Chapter 8:
You Can't Fly Money

**'There is a level of commitment that
you put into a passion that will
never be equaled in a hobby.'**
—Dave Romeo

On October 3, 2009, my best friend, Peter Nicholson, made an infrequent visit to Pennsylvania. Even though it was over an hour's drive to meet him, it was still considerably shorter than the four-hour plus commute to Long Beach, New York on Long Island.

The purpose for Peter's trip was a glider flying competition just outside of Reading, Pennsylvania. As you can see from his picture on the front cover of this book, the glider is bigger than him. This is something that Peter has been involved with since the seventies, and while I have seen him fly his planes before, I had never actually witnessed him compete in a flying competition. It was quite an eye-opening experience.

'What's the big deal?' I thought to myself. *'Why would a bunch of grown men drive through two states to stand around in a field to watch some toy planes do circles in the sky for a few minutes?'* It was not until Peter explained to me just what was involved that I began to understand and appreciate his passion for this endeavor. It was not just launching, flying, and landing the glider. It was keeping your glider flying in the air for a predetermined amount of time (in this case, eight minutes), avoiding any foreign contact, and landing intact within a four-foot circle in the vast field—oh, and with the nose of the glider as close as possible to a specific point in the center of the circle.

I did not understand all the nuances involved with finding thermals (concentrations of warm air rising over a specific area) which create lift for the engineless flying contraptions—thus extending their ability to remain airborne longer. This was an art form which required great concentration, judgment, decision-making, alternate strategies, and patience. It dawned on me that these were among many of the same abilities that I developed through my passion for bass fishing. That is what a true passion does—it challenges us to discover who we are and what we will learn so we can strive to be the best at what we pursue. *Selecting a passion is not important; what we become as a result of mastering it is everything.*

While I was at the flying field visiting Peter, a fellow glider flyer came over to lament a recent problem he encountered. Apparently, the man had purchased a Supra model glider, but he could not get it to fly properly. For some reason, he was not able to exchange the malfunctioning glider for a new one. While he said the merchant was willing to give him a refund, it was clear that the only thing that would satisfy this flying enthusiast was a properly working Supra glider. When I asked Peter privately why his friend did not just get a different model glider, he simply remarked in his unmistakable way, *'You can't fly money.'* I instantly understood his meaning. *Buying a fish* is in no way as satisfying as *catching a fish*. While the hobbyist would be financially reimbursed, his joy was only going to come from finding a working replacement Supra glider. Money had nothing to do with it.

That was a great day for me in that it answered a question that had gnawed at me for as long as I had known my friend: How could he have such a strong fascination in a passion for which I had no interest, and at the same time, why did he derive so little, if any, enjoyment on the few times when we fished together?

Has this ever happened to you? You have a friend who just loves being involved in something that you do not enjoy, but he or she cannot stop talking about it. Meanwhile, you realize that your friend does not share a very strong interest in a passion of yours. So how and why do you remain friends despite these different pursuits?

Peter and I have been best friends since the first day of eighth grade. We went through the same small private school together. We held several similar interests such as playing soccer and following hockey. Yet, we were definitely our own persons. He liked classical music, while I listened mostly to British Rock. He sang in a church choir while I played guitar in a cover band. He liked the New York Rangers, while I switched and became an Islanders fan when the franchise began to show some true promise in 1975. (I do not think he has ever completely forgiven me for that.) He threw himself into building and flying model planes, while I was consumed with bass fishing.

The answer comes down to respect for the person, for your differences, and for the commitment that a passion—really any passion—demands. One of the advantages of being friends with someone who truly excels at a passion you do not share is the exposure you get into different interests.

My parents loved to bowl, although it is not an activity my wife and I have ever done since we have known each other. Yet, my parents would update us whenever we would talk on how many points their team took, high games, and their league standings. My father was on a never-ending search to find *'the perfect bowling ball.'* Size, weight, finger holes; he was always looking for that ideal combination that would transform his game.

You can gain a great appreciation when you see someone you care about so immersed in a healthy, positive activity, even if you do not personally share it. Kim and I would politely listen to my parents bowling recaps just as they always asked me about my bass fishing status. It is the respect for that person you love—not the passion— that connects you.

It is that same healthy respect that has bound my friendship with Peter for the past 41 years. We are joined by our adolescent experiences, our friends, our families, our memories, and our mutual respect. He was the best man at our wedding in 1990. He was my best friend then and my best friend now. He is a friend in whom I can confide, whether we are talking about a shared passion, or an unshared one. Knowing that we accept each other for who we are, and being true to our own individual pursuits, has created a timeless friendship.

Many of the passions you pursue will not be about money, or recognition, or fame. Passions are vehicles which ignite our spirits. For example, I have painted the same outdoor statue of the Virgin Mary twice already, and will no doubt paint it again. My mother-in-law gave it to us. The first time I painted it, I neglected to put a varnish over the finished work to protect it from the elements when I put it outside. It had to be completely stripped and repainted from scratch because the finish had cracked due to the extremely hot and cold Pennsylvania temperature swings over a year's time.

While I did use a protective varnish on my second go-round, it left an unattractive stain over the newly repainted statue, undoing the four months of time I had invested in restoring it after my first failed attempt. Also, the paint cracked and even chipped off in some places, again from the elements.

I will surely end up repainting this same statue a third time; however not before thoroughly researching the right type of paint, varnish, and coating to protect it from the harsh northeastern weather conditions to which it will be exposed. I suppose I could just go out and get a similar pre-painted outdoor statue instead, but that would defeat the purpose of doing it myself, with my own two hands. After all…*you can't paint money either.* That would be like '*buying the trophy.*'

> *'I never did it because I needed it.*
> *I did it because I loved it…it's a passion.'*
> *—Paul McCartney*
> *(explaining why he continued to go on*
> *tour after he was rich and famous)*

Chapter 9:
Looking out my Back Door

*'Behold the birds of the air, for they
neither sow, nor do they reap, nor
gather into barns: and your heavenly
Father feedeth them. Are not you
of much more value than they?'*
—Matthew 6:26

In my last personal growth book *Striving for Significance*, I explained that when I stopped bass fishing, I looked for other passions with which to occupy my time. I once came across this proverb: *An hour of gardening is better than a medicine cabinet full of pills.* I thought perhaps maintaining our beautiful property would fill my angling void, but while I do not mind the activity, I can hardly claim it to be a passion. It did, however, put me in close proximity to develop a love of bird watching.

I will be the first to admit that growing up in New York, I never really paid much attention to birds. Around our house on Long Island, we really only saw robins, sparrows, and blue jays. Most of my free time was spent fishing so I was looking down at the water and was—for the most part—oblivious to any flying fowl overhead. About the only birds I encountered while fishing were ducks, swans, and geese. I did not care much for these birds because they were usually impeding where I wanted to fish, or were outwardly aggressive as they defended their nests or hatchlings. Even the random great blue heron was viewed only as a competitor for the same prime fishing spots. However, with change, occasionally comes maturity, and it was not until after I hung up my fishing rods that I acquired a greater appreciation for our feathered friends.

One day I was cleaning out the garage, and I came upon an unmarked and unopened cardboard box. I opened it up and discovered a bluebird house inside. I could not remember when we got it, but I knew we must have had it for a while. I showed it to Kim and she remembered that a friend of hers won it at a fundraiser and gave it to us. It had been in our garage for years. Of one thing I was certain—there were no bluebirds in our garage. Since I had learned that bluebirds like to feel secure in uncrowded surroundings, I found a place on our back fence where it could sit far enough away from any of our evergreen trees.

While I was aware that we had birds around the property, I never really paid much attention to what species of birds they were until I put up that birdhouse. Shortly after I did, Kim mentioned that she also had a hummingbird feeder in the garage which we had never hung up. I looked around the garage and located the hummingbird feeder box, only to discover that the glass cylinder had broken and was in numerous pieces inside the still closed box. I opted to throw it out, and instead, we purchased several feeders for different types of birds. Personally, it did not matter to me which ones we bought, but Kim, who knew much more about birds than I did, selected a Nyjer seed feeder for gold finches, a traditional feeder for cardinals and other birds, a suet block for woodpeckers, and a replacement hummingbird feeder.

So far we have discovered cardinals, blue jays, bluebirds, American goldfinches, dark-eyed juncos, thrashers, mourning doves, grackles, chickadees, cowbirds, catbirds, mockingbirds, tufted titmice, robins, downy woodpeckers, hairy woodpeckers, red-bellied woodpeckers, house finches, and sparrows feeding in our yard—and many of them just a few feet away from us on our deck.

In addition to the species of birds previously listed, the view from the sunroom door has afforded us front-row access to chipmunks, rabbits, deer, foxes, red tail hawks, turkey vultures, and bats.

As our bird watching fascination progressed, so did my ability to select certain blends of bird seed to attract specific types of birds. We have added to, and upgraded our bird feeders to reduce the intrusion of squirrels, and allow more birds to feed simultaneously. The addition of a birdbath on our deck nearly tripled the number of birds present at any one time. 30 birds frequently share the space, and take turns feeding themselves and their young, or splash with reckless abandon in the obliging pool of water.

How odd it is to think that there was a time when I could not discern the differences between one species and another. Now, I can easily distinguish between a red-headed house finch and my favorite, a brown thrasher. In fact, I often watch the mated pair, which reside on our property, scout for night crawlers and dazzle the eye with their colorful antics. I celebrate the brilliance of a male gold finch with its sweet warbling as it first approaches, and then again, just as it departs.

I see these birds on my commute to work as they playfully flit from one thistle plant to another in search of Nyjer seed or some other delicacy. I never noticed these most colorful creatures before 2008, yet I can pick out their call—sight unseen—as they fly overhead when I cross the street to retrieve my mail. So too, I revel in the gentility of a bluebird, the music of a courting robin red breast, and the sleekness of a catbird with its confident strut as it inspects our deck for its favorite seeds.

One particular characteristic that fascinates me about the male goldfinch is the way it interacts with people. This brilliant yellow parakeet-sized creature is very gentle in its movements. When Kim and I sit out in the evening on our deck, we are only about six feet away from our Nyjer seed feeder—a favorite landing site for gold finches.

For some reason, only the brightly-colored male gold finch is comfortable enough to land in our presence.

Without fail, the male bird approaches us singing its sweet song and continues only singing for a few seconds as if to make sure that we know he is there. Our little friend then stops singing and lands on the top of the feeder. He then makes his way down the feeder by walking sideways until it finds a nice place from which to feed. As it eats, it usually perches on the far side of the feeder so he can keep an eye on my wife and me, while he continues to enjoy his meal. After a few minutes of this posturing, the yellow bird settles down and will continue feeding, rarely ever checking to see if the Romeos have made any sudden moves (we do try to remain as still as possible during our feathered friends' welcomed evening visits).

The male gold finch generally gorges himself for about five minutes before he departs, and then, just as he does when he arrives, he serenades us as he gets ready to take flight. Perhaps it is his way of saying, *'Thank you for a lovely dinner.'* What a priceless experience to see how this amazing creature behaves and interacts with people.

As time progressed, our little friend brought his mate and their six new-born babies to join them on the Nyjer feeder. Often, they cannot all fit on the feeder at the same time. The young birds that had not yet learned how to balance on the Nyjer Seed feeder will often sit a few feet away on the deck or railing, flapping their newly-discovered wings, chirping the entire time, lest their parents forget how hungry the babies are. It truly is an incredibly touching sight.

It has become a reminder, during times of stress and uncertainty, just how much the simple pleasures of life can soothe even the most formidable challenges. It is amazing; the sense of serenity one experiences when you see how uncomplicated their existence is, and how we tend to overcomplicate our lives, worrying about trivial matters that cause us to lose sleep tonight, and yet, cannot even be remembered four months from now.

The male downy woodpecker, with its proud red patch and black and white speckled feathers, loves to pick a choice piece of suet from the blocks we keep caged and hanging from a metal stand on our deck, and then fly away to feast on it.

The grey and white mockingbird, which motions its tail feathers up and down prior to its take-offs, makes rare but welcome visits to our feeders, providing the suet block is to his liking. I never even knew that this was an actual species!

So what does bird-watching get you? What is the value of this passion? Do not look to a balance sheet for the answer. On the contrary, the 10-pound bags of birdseed became an additional expense we were not previously incurring. Still, it is considerably less-expensive than yacht racing *(or so I imagine)*. Does it make for intriguing conversations at social functions? Occasionally, but not extensively. It is usually only a passing mention to anyone not actually witnessing the experience. Does it provide valuable information? Perhaps if you are a contestant on *Jeopardy!* and the category is 'songs birds of Central Pennsylvania,' but the odds of this happening are rather slim.

The true value comes from the shared time and connection with my wife, Kim, as we commune with nature, just inches away from our dining room. The intimate exposure to these fascinating creatures has changed me—for the better. I no longer need to *'be'* somewhere else, to be content and at peace. The juxtaposition of nature in such close proximity to the comfort of our home has combined the best of both worlds.

There exists now, a purity of thought and a greater clarity of purpose, intermingled with the love and appreciation for the wonder of nature and the magnificence of God—and I am awestruck by the pairing.

If this appeals to you, you can gaze upon your own unique collections of birds in your region. The species will vary, but the experience will be similar. You can enjoy hours of peaceful contemplation of nature, and the harmony and simplicity of animals that coexist and share the same feeding area. One of the privileges of having a passion like bird-watching is that it can be a simple pleasure that is its own reward. Perhaps it is the fact that, at least in our case, bird-watching is a nearly effortless activity, which we can enjoy and experience year-round with no travel time, no travel costs, or pre-planning. It is immediately rewarding and fulfilling, and restores serenity in the midst of life's challenges.

Dave Romeo

'SKIRTING the river road,
(my forenoon walk, my rest,)
Skyward in air a sudden muffled sound,
the dalliance of the eagles,
The rushing amorous contact
high in space together,
The clinching interlocking claws,
a living, fierce, gyrating wheel,
Four beating wings, two beaks,
a swirling mass tight grappling,
In tumbling turning clustering loops,
straight downward falling,
Till o'er the river pois'd, the twain yet one,
a moment's lull,
A motionless still balance in the air,
then parting, talons loosing,
Upward again on slow-firm pinions
slanting, their separate diverse flight,
She hers, he his, pursuing.'
—Walt Whitman
(from 'The Dalliance of the Eagles' Leaves of Grass)

60

Chapter 10:
Let's Talk Sports

*'When I was about 18, and my dad
and I couldn't communicate about
anything at all, we could still talk
about baseball. Now, that was real!'*
—Daniel Stern
(Phil Berquist in the movie, City Slickers)

I must admit that high school was not my favorite time. Since I was attending a private school eight miles away, I was usually the first student picked up in the morning and the last student dropped off in the afternoon. I really hated getting up so early, especially to get dressed to go to school. However, my two best friends were there, so I knew at least that I would have some fun with them. One of our favorite school activities was playing soccer. Now this I did like. In fact you might say, *we lived for soccer* and looked forward to it during the first few months of each new school year.

I was actually pretty good, and scored a lot of goals, but one thing really frustrated me—our coach. For some reason, he tended to favor one of the other players over me. Whenever the other player scored two goals in a game, he would keep him in so he could get a *'hat trick'* (score three goals in the same game). That was fine with me; however, whenever I scored two goals in the same game, the coach would pull me out and say *'Let someone else get a chance to play.'* This would irritate me to no end, but there was nothing I could really do about it.

In 1973, our league—comprised of six private schools—decided to have an all-star soccer game, where the best players from five teams would play the the number-one-ranked-team in our league, Woodmere Academy. I wanted to be in that game so bad I could taste it. Both Peter Nicholson and I knew that if we were to make the team, we would have to be in third place in our league. In the game, just before the all-star game, our team fell behind one to nothing. Peter and I just looked at each other and knew, if we were going to be in the all-star game, we had to win this game. Working together, with almost telepathic understanding and anticipation of the other's moves, Peter scored the tying goal and I scored the game winner. We were going onto the all-star game!

What I looked forward to most was that, since our team finished third, it meant that our coach would not be coaching the all-star team. That duty fell instead to the second place team's coach. He wanted to win as much as Peter and I did, so the coach let me play until the end of the game. We won 3-0, and I scored the first two goals and assisted on the third. I was named Most Valuable Player of the game. I felt validated, not having my own coach holding back my success.

I doubt that anyone—but Peter and I—even remembers that game. It was so long ago and it really does not have much relevance to anyone else. The reason that game meant so much to me was because it was the first time I ever had a coach demonstrate how much he believed in me and allowed me to discover my potential at a sport in which I excelled. I learned that a great coach does not stifle, but rather encourages you to bring forth your best effort. It was not just important for my own personal growth, but it planted the seed for my role as a results coach, which I have now been doing since 1998. I remember what it meant to have someone believe in me and root for my success. This is my role when working with my coaching clients. The two phrases that I repeat the most often when I coach someone are, *'I believe in you'*, and *'I am rooting for you'*. I believe my passion for success in soccer has made me a better results coach today.

Still, unless you are captivated by a particular sport, you may be completely oblivious to its beneficial qualities. I must admit that growing up, it was hard for me to comprehend how a group of grown men, wearing white, pinstriped uniforms could be paid so much money for hitting a little ball across a baseball field. It made no sense to my young mind. There were wars, hunger, diseases, and social ills. Why did baseball players, football players, and basketball players make so much more money than surgeons, soldiers, missionaries, and teachers? What value does throwing an odd-shaped ball down the length of a field to gain a few yards produce? How does throwing a big orange ball through a hoop do anything to save the world? How does swatting a little white, dimpled, golf ball save even one life? How are these contributing to society?

To me they just seemed like such frivolous activities. I thought to myself, *'Shouldn't we be taking care of more serious problems like the breakdown of the family, protecting our freedom, and reducing crime?'* Have you ever asked yourself these or similar questions?

The reality is we *should* be working on restoring the family unit, securing our borders, protecting our sovereignty, and making citizens safe. And while we endeavor in these noble pursuits, we should continue to throw a ball, swing a golf club, and sink the five-ball in the left-side pocket.

It took me years to realize that there is a very strong relationship between watching the New York Yankees rally in the ninth inning to pull off a come from behind World Series victory, and dealing with serious real-world problems.

Human beings are human. They require rest and release in order to perform their best. In the movie *The Ten Commandments*, Moses is criticized by his rival, the Pharaoh's son, for being too soft on the Hebrew slaves charged with building a city. He had opened up the Egyptian grain stores for the slaves, and gave them one day a week to rest and worship. Moses justifies his decisions by saying, *'Cities are made of bricks. The strong make many. The weak make few. The dead make none.'*

Moses got it. Do you? We are not slaves. It is true that we *work to live,* but we do not *live to work.* We must have healthy diversions to handle the stress of life. Why do so many doctors play golf? It seems like such a pointless pursuit. That is—in part—its appeal and its purpose. It can be light, and pleasant, and meaningless in comparison to performing surgery to remove a cancerous brain tumor. Consider this; if you were the patient, awaiting this difficult procedure, wouldn't you want your surgeon to be completely unstressed and focused while performing this operation?

This is the value of sports. Physical stress can relieve mental stress in a healthy way. If you play a sport, you will probably feel physically drained following the activity. You will also gain a shared bonding experience with your teammates as you reflect on the incredible feats that can be accomplished when talent, desire, selflessness, discipline, and commitment come together. It is true; the whole is indeed, greater than the sum of its parts. The camaraderie created by giving your all in a common pursuit is often the most rewarding aspect of the game.

If you go to a stadium to watch a football game, you will drink in all of the sights, sounds, and smells associated with the experience of being part of the event.

I never enjoyed a hot dog more than at Shea Stadium watching the New York Mets while my grandfather and I would celebrate our shared birthday, August 7, see our names up on the scoreboard, and get a complimentary ice cream cake. What a day! What special memories! And while my grandfather is gone, those special days have lived on in my memory for over 40 years.

Even if you watch sports at home, you will often find it can be a great bonding experience for you, your family, or your friends. Men especially enjoy *'shoulder to shoulder'* activities like watching a sporting event together. You are living it out together. You experience the glorious highpoints simultaneously as they transpire and become part of your collective history. The beauty of being an *'armchair quarterback'* is that it does not require you to be in perfect health or of playing age to enjoy.

Have you ever listened to a sports announcer? Notice how much passion, emotion, and enthusiasm they muster to do the play-by-play coverage of an event you cannot see. Even if someone is confined to a wheelchair, has Downs Syndrome, cannot see, or may be lying in a hospital bed, he or she can still enjoy listening to a well-called ballgame over the radio.

Soldiers in war zones want to know the score of their favorite team. It serves to keep them grounded when everything around them is in total chaos. It reconnects them with the world, and the way of life they are fighting to preserve. It almost does not matter what the score is, just the fact that somewhere, in this crazy world, there remains something worth going back home to experience. *It is hope.*

I remember hearing Sean Hannity once say that he loves watching any top performing sporting competition—like the World Series, or the Super Bowl—because there is something very special about seeing the absolute best in their field rise to the occasion and give their all. I understand this observation and share the sentiment. It creates a unity of pride among the citizens of the winning team's city, and sometimes, even the entire state.

Look at the sense of national pride when our nation's best take home Olympic gold medals. That is why we pay attention to the medal counts. Athletics can bring together an entire nation.

In addition, professional sports generates an enormous economic boom, providing a ripple effect of opportunities and jobs, including ticket takers, travel agents, advertising agencies, food vendors, marketing companies, trainers, security services, hoteliers, gas station attendants, airline workers, bankers, accountants, entertainers, doctors, clean-up crews, broadcasters, television crews, merchandisers, printers, statisticians, coaches, general managers, talent scouts, camera operators, organists, and restaurateurs.

So in essence, maybe football *can save the economy!* I suppose it is possible that a round of golf *can save lives!* And perhaps the Olympics *can help win a World War.* The point is, your passion for sports may be fulfilling a much greater positive and meaningful purpose than you realize. That is all the more reason to play full out when pursuing your passion in a sports capacity. Your success may have a more far-reaching impact on inspiring others to greatness.

In wrapping up this chapter, I want to share one last anecdote about athletics with you. While visiting some family members in Conroe, Texas in 2010, I stopped in to spend some time with my Uncle Michael and Aunt Margaret.

As I walked into their living room for the very first time, I was struck by a beautiful framed photograph of my cousin, Tori Klabunde, in mid-flight as she was engaged in a ring jump as part of a gymnastics competition.

I learned that Tori's dedication to gymnastics and cheerleading required her to practice 24 hours a week (mostly from 4:30-9:00 PM plus Saturday mornings) including travel time to and from school. Her mother, Maria, would drive so Tori could do her homework in the car en route to practice. I thought to myself, *'I wonder how many other seventh-graders—never mind professional athletes—would be willing to commit to this grueling routine?* I also imagined, *'If this is how hard the girls have to work to make the cheerleading squad, the football team must have some of the most incredible players in the world!'*

I asked Tori what she got out of gymnastics and why she picked that passion. She said, *'I gained my athletic physique, dedication, perseverance, self-confidence, and commitment (through gymnastics). It taught me never to give up on myself.'*

Awestruck at the extension of Tori's arms, legs, neck, spine, and torso, it was obvious to me that this photo had to be included on the cover of this book. As you can see from her image, she has thoroughly thrown herself into her passion. It personifies what it means to truly commit all you have in the pursuit of your passion.

> *'We read poetry because we are members*
> *of the human race and the human race*
> *is filled with passion. Medicine, law,*
> *business, engineering—these are noble*
> *pursuits and necessary to sustain life.*
> *But poetry, beauty, romance, love—*
> *these are the things we stay alive for.'*
> *—John Keating*
> *(Robin Williams in the movie Dead Poets Society)*

Chapter 11:
It's a Great Day for Hockey!

'The most dangerous position in
hockey is a three-goal lead.'
—Old hockey proverb

In 2009, the Pittsburgh Penguins won their third Stanley Cup championship. In 2010, the Pittsburgh Steelers won their fifth Super Bowl championship. The city, which was in financial ruin just a few years earlier, was now being billed as the *'City of Champions.'*

Kim and I came to love hockey from two different directions—decades apart. In 1971, I started going to a private school in eighth grade called Saint Andrews Episcopal School in Oceanside, NY on Long Island. What I soon discovered was that, while I was attending, six different New York Rangers (Vic Hadfield, Bruce MacGregor, Brad Park, Dale Rolfe, Bobby Rousseau, and Walter Tkazcuk) had children enrolled in that same school. Although most of the kids were significantly younger than me, many of my schoolmates were die-hard Rangers fans (notice I did not say '*hockey*' fans).

One of my two best friends (mentioned earlier in chapter 8), Peter Nicholson, was completely to blame for introducing me to this sport. Peter lived in Long Beach, as did many of the Rangers players. Since Peter's father was a doctor, he often treated many of the players in his home practice. Thus, the Nicholson family was immersed in the NY Rangers. Peter and his four brothers all played ice hockey. Since they ranged in age from about nine to 15 years old at the time, they played on different teams, in different leagues, and at different times.

Picture this: If you are in an ice hockey league, you play in a public ice hockey rink. You have to wait until the rinks are closed to the general public but opened to the league teams for practices and games. That meant that your playing time could be between 10:00 PM and 2:00 AM. Since most of the games took place during school nights, the boys would set their alarm clocks to wake up in enough time to get ready and go to the rink.

As our friendship grew, I began to stay over at Peter's house and the Nicholsons became like my second family. Sometimes, the alarm clock would go off at midnight, and we would all get dressed as Mrs. Nicholson would transport Peter, his older brother, Denis, and me to the rink for a one o'clock game. When it was over, she would drive us back to their home. Within minutes of hitting the beds they were asleep. In fact, I discovered the very

next day on the bus that Peter had acquired the skill of
sleeping standing up or anywhere he was, to catch up on
his sleep. While this was all new to me, the Nicholsons
were used to this routine. On different nights, Mrs.
Nicholson would drive her other sons in other leagues
to their games.

When the Rangers played, it was a family event. Unless it was your turn to use the family's season tickets to
see the game live at Madison Square Garden, the Nicholsons would gather around their living room television
set and watch the game.

I remember the first hockey game I ever attended. It
was the 26th National Hockey League (NHL) All-star
game at Madison Square Garden on January 30, 1973.
Peter had two tickets that his father got from one of the
players. We were sitting next to Steve Vickers, a Rangers
player who was injured at the time. It was such a new
and overwhelming experience. I was hooked. I became a
Rangers fan, and even took up ice hockey to play on the
same team with Peter, Denis, and my other best friend,
Art Gardner. I only played that one year, so I did not
really get very good at it. Luckily, the team had enough
talent without me to win the championship that year.

While I did not continue to play ice hockey, I still
loved watching it. But the Rangers were a painfully poor
team to root for at that time, and I soon grew tired of
watching *the agony of defeat*—a term I am sure was first
coined by Rangers fans. I started following the New
York Islanders, who had only come into the league in
1972. Peter and his family considered me a traitor for

switching my allegiance, but I saw the desire and determination of the Islanders players of the time, and the team played at the Nassau Coliseum on Long Island, which was within walking distance of my house. The Islanders started off with one of the worst seasons in NHL history. I can still remember John, one of Peter's younger brothers, once chuckling, '*Wouldn't it be funny if the Islanders won the Stanley Cup before the Rangers!*' While it sounded like sheer lunacy at the time, it seemed almost prophetic in hindsight. Only seven years after the team's founding, the New York Islanders went on to their first Stanley Cup championship!

May 24, 1980—I can still remember it as if it were yesterday. The unthinkable was about to happen. The lowly New York Islanders—who started off their first season with one of the worst records in NHL history— were playing the 2-time Stanley Cup winning Philadelphia Flyers in game six of the Stanley Cup finals. It was a Saturday afternoon and I was listening to the game in my car because I was working as a driver at Chicken Delight in Westbury, Long Island that day. I hoped the game would be over before I had to go to work, but the game was tied 4-4 and went into sudden death overtime.

I was making deliveries to people's houses. I was afraid that when I shut off my car to make the next delivery, I would miss a crucial part of the game. Just as I pulled up to my next house, I heard the announcer yell, '*Score!*' as Bobby Nystrom put the game-winning goal into the Flyers' net. I could not believe it! I was yelling

'Score!' at the top of my lungs. Unfortunately, I had just turned the ignition key to off, out of reflex, before I started screaming, and of course, my car windows were rolled down.

The people in the house saw this 22-year-old delivery boy screaming like a maniac in front of their home. I do not believe they were hockey fans, and they certainly did not know why I was yelling. All I can say is, it was a good thing I was bringing them food.

What an incredible time it was for Long Island. The New York Islanders went on to win four consecutive Stanley Cup championships and it was one of the happiest sports memories of my life. We got spoiled going to the *'annual'* Stanley Cup championship parade every year, at least for a while.

Unfortunately, the Dynasty came to an end in 1984. While I still followed the Islanders, they too became disappointing, and over the last 28 years, have never been in serious Stanley Cup contention.

After getting married and moving to Pennsylvania in 1990, my hockey interest waned—not because I did not enjoy the sport, but because in Central PA, hockey was pretty much a forgotten sport. There were no local NHL teams, and games were rarely ever televised in our area.

But all that changed in 1997 when we moved one town west to Elizabethtown, PA and were eligible to get Fox Sports Network Pittsburgh (FSN). As soon as Kim discovered we could get the Pittsburgh Penguins hockey games, our viewing habits changed in a major way. The

Penguins had won their first two Stanley Cup Championships in the early nineties. Kim was instantly a fan of the Penguins and, I was eager to follow.

When I told some friends earlier this year that we drove to Pittsburgh to go to a Penguins game to celebrate Kim's birthday, they thought I was being selfish in my selection of activity until they realized that this was her choice. She claims it was the best birthday she ever had. If I had a head start over Kim in my fascination with hockey, she certainly closed the gap with her thorough knowledge of the players, the rules, the standings, and prospective draft picks.

Kim is incredibly focused on the team's status, and frequently checks the Penguins' website and e-mails for the latest updates about the team. She also keeps the Penguins' scores and statistics throughout the entire season, including shutouts and hat tricks.

Our interest and dedication really grew in 2009, and was rewarded when the Pittsburgh Penguins won their third Stanley Cup championship. Kim and I saw every game that year. We were riveted to the television. Having seen the Penguins go down to defeat at the hands of the Detroit Red Wings in game 7 of the 2008 Stanley Cup finals, we could not miss the rematch the next year against the same team. It went down to the wire—another game 7 decision, with the final game played in the Motor City.

The Penguins had a 2-0 lead going into the final period. The Red Wings scored with six minutes and seven seconds remaining in the third period, making the rest of the game a real nail biter. With six and a half seconds remaining, Detroit won a faceoff in the Penguins' end of the ice. When Nicklas Lidstrom took his wrist shot from only 10 feet away from the net, I was sure he would tie the game, forcing a sudden death overtime finish. Yet, somehow, the Penguins goaltender, Marc Andre Fleury, thrust his body forward to prevent the puck from going in net, and the Pittsburgh Penguins held on to win their third Stanley Cup.

What is different about Penguins hockey from any of the other teams I followed is the overwhelming experience of *being immersed* in the team. There exists a symbiotic relationship among the team, the management, the staff, and the fans. When you go to a Pittsburgh Penguins game, you are decked out from head to toe in every conceivable article of clothing that can have a Penguins logo slapped on it. Why do you do this? Partly because when you go to a Pittsburgh Penguins game, you are surrounded by over 18,000 other fans who are also decked out from head to toe in every conceivable article of clothing that can have a Penguins logo slapped on it. And partly it is because part of the Penguins experience is the identification with the team. I have never seen this done to this degree with any other professional sports franchise.

Still, there is so much more to the Pittsburgh Penguins organization than just the on-ice play. It is the team's captain, Sidney Crosby, who, along with other players, personally delivers season tickets to die-hard Penguins fans.

There is George, one of the greeters at the Consol Energy Center (the Penguins home-ice arena), who stands outside the building before the games, watching for people like Kim (who has an artificial knee and uses a cane when she attends the games). As George has previously instructed me, I pull up in front of the arena so Kim can get out and George escorts her into the building while I park the car across the street. Meanwhile, Canon, one of the ushers, brings Kim's wheelchair and transports her to our seats, and then like clockwork after the game, he is waving and waiting at the top of our gate to take Kim back down to the closest point to our car. Is it any wonder why the Penguins' home-game sell-out streak is now over five-years long?

It is people like the late Kenny Geidel, a.k.a. *the Cotton Candy Guy,* who was such a beloved fixture of the Penguins organization that there are numerous You-Tube videos where fans had their pictures taken in frame while Kenny made his unmistakable announcements of *'Cotton Candy, here!'* I once mentioned to Kenny that we could often pick out his voice when we watch the Penguins home games on television. He said, *'Yes, other people have told me that too.'* He will be missed.

It is the video clip of Hulk Hogan saying *'Whatcha gonna do when Malkamania runs wild on you, brother?'* that plays every time Penguins center Evgeni Malkin scores a goal on home ice.

It is people like cancer survivor, Cy Clark, *the Malkamania Guy,* who dresses up at every home game like Hulk Hogan wearing sunglasses, a doo-rag, and a black and gold feathered boa, and leads the crowd in cheers whenever one of the players scores a goal. By the way, if you have never been to Pittsburgh, black and gold are the official colors of the city and its three professional sports teams; The Steelers (football), The Pirates (baseball), and the Penguins (hockey—*Weren't you paying attention!*)

It is *the Knitting Lady* who brings her chartreuse-colored sign that says, *'The Knitting Lady says Let's Go Pens!'* and displays it whenever she is caught on camera for television or the *jumbo-tron.* Of course, holding up her sign does not interrupt her from continuing to engage in her other passion—knitting—which she does before, during, and after the game.

It is sportscaster Mike Lange, who's corny clichés are spit out in his gravely, emotion-packed voice whenever a Penguins player scores a goal. These classic sayings are now marketed on everything from t-shirts to rings tones for your phone. These include, *'Scratch my back with a hacksaw', 'Tell Arnold Slick from Turtle Crick', 'Oh Michael, Michael, Motorcycle', 'He beat him like a rented mule', 'Let's go hunt moose on a Harley', 'He's smiling like a butcher's dog',* and *'Elvis has just left the building'.*

It is events like *the Shirts off their backs fan appreciation day.* After the very last regular season home game, each of the Pittsburgh Penguins players (even if they are injured, or did not dress for that game) come out wearing nice clean jerseys, pose for a picture with a different fan (selected earlier in a random drawing), sign the jersey, and give it to that fan.

And it is far more than a game or a sport. It is a connection. It is almost like speaking another language. I know people who *'speak hockey.'* We can talk for hours when we meet about all things hockey—players, plays, games, trades, injuries, draft picks, slumps, strategies, coaches, rules, statistics, predictions, etc. It is rare in Central Pennsylvania to find someone who *speaks hockey*, which makes those occasions all the more special. It is rarer still to find someone who *speaks fluent Penguins*.

One evening, while Kim and I were dining at Arthur's Restaurant in the Eden Resort, I took out my wallet to pay for our meal. Mike Tyson, our server, noticed the distinctive black and gold Penguins logo on my wallet and immediately began asking us if we had seen the game the night before (as if we would miss one!). He continued to discuss the goaltender's play, a particularly great goal scored, their playoff chances, and many other nuances of the game.

It is an anticipated relief from the grinding pace of an exceptionally grueling week, knowing that you can go home and escape for a few hours, enthralled in the action-packed competition of another Penguins game. There are times when I live to see the next game.

It is also a bridge—a connection. On those times when Kim and I are at odds with each other over one thing or another, there is always the Penguins. It is a neutral topic where we can both converse comfortably at length in minute detail, and get right with each other once again. Now how can you beat that? It is a shared point of reference with our friends and family members, spread far and wide, who also understand and appreciate how a sport—and a shared passion—can unite a couple, a family, and a city. *Let's go Pens!*

'You miss 100% of the shots you don't take.'
—Wayne Gretsky

Chapter 12:
The Sound of Music

'If music be the food of love, play on.'
—William Shakespeare
(Duke Orsino from Twelfth Night Act: 1 Scene: 1)

There was a time when music consumed my every waking thought. Whether it was listening to music, seeing a live concert, writing music, learning how to play someone else's music on the guitar, performing in a cover band, or writing my own songs, music became one of the strongest focuses in my life, as a means of staving off the mundane. Some of those memories were so profound that I can still recall many vivid details of the events even now. One such memory is when I saw Led Zeppelin in concert for the very first time in 1975.

I started going to concerts in 1973, so I had probably only been to about 20 by the time I first saw Led Zeppelin live. They were the biggest band on the planet at that time, and at the height of their popularity. When they came to the Nassau Coliseum, their concert sold out immediately, and I did not have a ticket. Living close to the Nassau Coliseum, I went there one day to buy tickets for another concert, and I casually asked the ticket seller if there were any tickets left for Led Zeppelin. He said, *'The first show is sold out, but a second show was just added for February 14. It is on sale now.'* I could not believe it, so I bought four tickets for Led Zeppelin on the spot.

I went with Peter Nicholson's brother, Denis, Laura Hetterick, and Karen Omundsen, two of the girls from our high school class. We were all very big Led Zeppelin fans so we could not wait for the concert. To this day, I can still remember every song they played. They opened with *Rock and Roll,* continued with *Sick Again, Over the Hills and Far Away, In My Time of Dying, Since I've Been Loving You, The Song Remains the Same* segued into *The Rain Song, Kashmir, No Quarter, Trampled Underfoot, Moby Dick, Dazed and Confused,* and *Stairway to Heaven,* with *Whole Lotta Love,* and *Heartbreaker* as the encore.

It was about as picture perfect a performance as you could have imagined. Jimmy Page, who played with a broken finger, which he caught in a closing train door a month earlier, was incredible. To this day, I have never seen anyone who could play a guitar with such incredible skill and control. The lightshow was one of the best, and the tightness of the band was unbelievable. It made me want to play guitar, to write music, to perform live in front of an audience, and to reach, move, and inspire people emotionally through my talents.

I followed through and became a guitar player and played in a band. Although I was not as skilled as I would have liked to become, I did learn a valuable lesson through this experience. I was the only member of the band who was 18 years old, which meant that we could not play in clubs because they served alcohol. About the only paying jobs we could get were birthday parties and battle of the band competitions. The battle of the band competitions only paid if you won first place.

In our first competition, our bass player broke his hand a week before the event, and we had to drop out. I am so glad we did! The other bands were far superior to us in skill and talent. It would have been a humiliating disaster had we played. One thing I noticed was that the first band that played did a great set, had the best equipment, and played superbly. I thought they would be a shoe-in to win. However, a three-piece band finished up the night. They were so tight. They played some songs from Peter Frampton's very popular new album *Frampton Comes Alive,* which had just recently been released, and the crowd went wild. I watched as this last band swept all the momentum from that first band, and won the competition in a landslide. What I learned from that night, and have never forgotten, is that sometimes *it is better to be last than to be the best.*

I used this strategy as my band progressed and got better—perhaps even, dare I say it—*good.* As the band manager, I handled all of the bookings. When we were next approached to do a battle of the bands, I agreed, provided we could go on last. Since none of the other bands had made such a request, the event promoter had no problem awarding us *the clean-up spot.*

A funny thing happened that night. The first band again was quite good with great equipment, good singing, and skilled musicians. They were probably the best band of the four. They played a good set, and closed with *Free Bird* by Lynryd Skynyrd. (If you are unfamiliar with this song, it is about four days long and very repetitious).

The second band played next. They were not as good as the first band and I really do not remember what they played—except that they too closed with *Free Bird*. By the time the third band launched into the—now even more familiar than before the competition—Lynryd Skynyrd anthem, people began coming up to us shaking their heads pleading, *'You're not going to play Free Bird, are you?'*

The fact is, we were planning to play *Free Bird* that night, but because we went last, we had the luxury of changing our minds (and our closing number) to *Rock and Roll* by Led Zeppelin. The crowd went crazy! They nearly started a riot to the point where the event promoter had to ask everyone to leave the building. He actually had to mail us the prize money because he could not control the crowd long enough that night to award us first place.

What I took from that experience was that whenever it came time to do a battle of the bands competition, our one stipulation was that we play last—and we never lost a battle of the bands competition.

Another memorable day took place in 1981, when some friends and I made a road trip to see the Rolling Stones at JFK Stadium in Philadelphia.

It was September 26, 1981, and although I had seen the Rolling Stones in concert before, this was different because it was a road trip with a bunch of the guys. In this instance, the guys included four of my guitar students, and Jimmy Madonna and Tony Daddio, both of whom I worked with at Chicken Delight. We drove down from Long Island at the crack of dawn to make sure we would reach JFK Stadium in Philadelphia, and still have enough time to find some seats, to watch the opening acts of George Thorogood and the Destroyers, and Journey, and to await the headliners.

When the guys showed up at my house early that morning, one of my students brought a box of doughnuts, and Jimmy came bearing a big bucket of fried chicken. It was just so great to see a bunch of people who did not know each other come together with such a positive outgoing friendly attitude, and treat one another as if they were lifelong friends.

The reason this day was so memorable was not because of the concert per se—although it was probably one of the best of the seven Rolling Stones concerts I have attended. It was the atmosphere—a road trip to Philadelphia with some of my favorite friends and clients who would not have otherwise known each other if they did not know me. And even if they did, they would most likely never have put this road trip together had I not organized it.

Anyone who has ever been to my seminars will understand why this is so important to me—it showed me that I had a gift for event planning and bringing together great people who have a fantastic time sharing a memorable experience. This carried over when I did bass fishing tournaments, and continues today in my seminars where the level of respect, professionalism, warmth, excitement, and fun are at the very heart of my seminars.

However, I began to grow tired of what I saw happening with many of the musicians to whom I looked up, or with whom I performed. Whether it was the sinful excesses in alcohol, drugs, bad behavior, or the ungodly content of the songs, I could see that these worldly vices were heading in a different direction from my values and my faith. I got so turned off that in 1981, I got rid of my entire rock and roll record collection in one day. I also stopped performing in my cover band.

And while I lost my interest in hard rock, I cannot deny the impact some of those events had on me until this day, when as a motivational speaker, I still enjoy the privilege of writing lesson plans, presenting live seminars in front of an audience, and reaching, moving, and inspiring people emotionally through my talents. I just found a better vehicle through which to express my passion for inspiring others.

Yet, even before that happened, my abandonment of rock music led me to pursue another artistic passion.

> *'Until you make peace with who you are you will never be content with what you have.'*
> *—Doris Mortman*

Chapter 13:
When I Paint My Masterpiece

'There is so much opportunity in life to pour yourself into the beauty of natural things. They surround us and inspire us to develop our contributions. Are you expressing your passion for the pure joy of life? Painting is a way of communicating your love of beauty with the world.'
—Pablo Picasso

You may find that over the years, your passions have overlapped at times. Sometimes one will rise while a previous one wanes. And on some rare occasions, your passions combine in the most delightful and rewarding ways.

Tossing out all of my rock albums in 1981 created a gaping void in my time and activities. I listened mostly to Broadway soundtrack albums and Frank Sinatra music, but no longer going to concerts left me with much more idle time to fill.

Eventually I began painting statues. I was pleasantly surprised to discover that I was fairly good at it. I threw myself into this activity because I loved it and because in some way, I believed it gave me a chance to atone from my previous involvement with hard rock music.

My first project was a plastic, sand-filled statue of the Blessed Mother, which we had in our backyard. At first, I thought I would just paint it three colors; blue, white, and gold. When I was done, I found that the paint I had used was not designed for outdoor plastic statues. The extreme summer heat caused the paint to expand and stretch, giving the Blessed Mother a less than holy appearance.

I did not mind repainting the statue (with the appropriate paints) because, from the time I finished painting it the first time, I kept thinking about how much better it would have looked if I had used more than three colors. So the second paint job was far superior to the first.

As I was working on this statue, relatives and family friends who visited our home commented favorably about my painting. (It really was not hard to make a plain white statue more attractive by adding a splash of color).

One day, my mother said that one of her friends mentioned she had an old statue that her mother had given her that was now in very poor condition, and wanted to know if I would restore and repaint it. That became my next project.

It was more complex than the first, as I had to learn how to use plaster, with just the right amount of water, to form a missing hand and nose. The local craft store employees were very helpful, and grateful to assist *their newest, steady customer,* which insured many repeat purchases of paint, brushes, and related art supplies.

My mother's friend was delighted with the results, and before I could even return the finished item back to her, I received another request from someone else. I did not take any money for my work for several reasons. First, at the very beginning, I was still learning and did not feel my work was good enough to charge for it. Second, I would not have known what to charge even if I did. Third, painting was a labor of love and I was enjoying this positive activity so much. It really helped me fill the void left by my abandonment of rock music. And fourth—and most importantly, I really looked at some of the improved work as being divinely influenced. God seemed to be directing my hands to accomplish things I cannot otherwise explain. In fact, I never signed my own name to any statue I painted, but instead left three initials *H.M.S.* on the bottom each piece which stood for *'His Master's Servant.'*

As the word spread among our family, friends, and acquaintances, I soon had a waiting list of people and statues in need of restoring and repainting. Coincidentally, almost all of the statues I restored were of a religious nature. My mother gave me the Holy Family statue her mother had given her. There were many busts of Christ, a Saint Michael statue, and an Infant of Prague.

I would pick up prayer cards at our church to learn, not only more about how the subjects should appear, but also about the lives of the saints and their significance in history. I discovered by painting these statues, that the subjects were often depicted wearing very specific colors and appeared with certain items.

For example, I learned that Saint Jude is *the Patron Saint of lost causes and desperate situations.* The statue of Saint Jude has him dressed in a green outer garment (depicting everlasting life) and white robe, distinguishing him as one of the twelve apostles. He is standing with a large stone-studded wooden club at his side, which represents one of the weapons used on him during his martyrdom. He also has a gold medallion on his chest, with the image of Jesus, referencing the legend of the Image of Edessa. There is also a flame of fire protruding from his head which signifies his presence at Pentecost, when he received the Holy Ghost with the other apostles.

As I previously stated, one passion can give rise to another. I was no longer just applying primer, paint, and glaze to preserve these ceramic icons—I was growing in the understanding and appreciation of my faith.

The culmination of passions for painting, bass fishing, and writing music resulted in the following song lyrics—one of the only songs in which I felt was divinely inspired.

I Just Hold the Brush

I can't paint a masterpiece
to captivate your eyes.

To say these talents are my own,
you know I'm telling lies.

I don't hold the power over what you'll see.

I just hold the brush He guides for me.

And I don't catch the fish you
see that overflow my boat.

And I can't calm the swirling
waves to keep my craft afloat.

No I don't have the pow'r to
still the raging sea.

I just hold the rod He guides for me.

All these talents come from God
and graciously were given.

And so I ply them every day
and hope to be forgiven.

And can't write the songs you hear
that send you to the moon.

I take none of the glory for
the lyrics or the tune.

No I know better than to claim this melody.

I just hold the pen He guides for me.

When I occasionally got caught up on restoring old, damaged statues, I began to take on other projects, like buying new, unpainted statues from my local craft store. The more I painted, the better I got, and I could see a distinctive style developing. While many of the similar finished pieces I examined showed light and dark shadings painted on solid garments and blended color to depict hair, I avoided these practices because, as three-dimensional objects, I felt that light—rather than paint—would more naturally accomplish the same effect. Also, I took great pride in making sure that even though items on plaster were all molded one onto the other, all items would be depicted with clear and distinctive colors separating one from the next, so no matter what angle you viewed the statue, the colors would be geometrically perfect. Also, since the statues were three-dimensional, I saw no reason that the underside of the statues should not also be painted and glazed.

Eventually, I began seeking out even bigger challenges. My *reticular activating system* was creating a greater awareness of statues. At church, I found myself being consumed with the distinctive statues on either side of the altar. I noticed that the large statue of Saint Joseph was in sorry shape, due to its continuous transport to and from a temporary location. The statue was chipped, and had broken off fingers and parts of a staff.

I asked one of our priests if I could restore the statue. He said it would be all right provided that I had it back and in place for the following Sunday Mass. That meant that I would have slightly less than one week to paint this four-foot tall, damaged statue, and return it to its proper setting.

I remember the challenges that came with this particular statue. For example, because of the sheer size, I had to make sure I had enough of each color paint to cover the corresponding surface. Holding and painting a statue of this size was also a challenge because of its weight and awkwardness.

Nothing could be done until the missing extremities were molded, dried, and checked for cracks. This was very difficult, as I was building items for which I had no model. I had to visualize the missing parts, and extrapolate how the original fingers would look and bend—if they were still attached to the statue. Chips and nicks were filled in and smoothed over before the base coat could be applied.

By the time every missing piece was restored, I had about three days left to complete all of the painting. When it comes to painting statues, you usually start with the lightest colors like white first. This way, when you add a darker color and touch the lighter one, the original color does not show through. You can only handle the unpainted or dry parts of the statue as you turn it and apply additional paint. This usually requires you to take breaks as the paint dries—causing greater downtime. For me, touch-ups, especially on the face, lips, hair, and eyes, are the most challenging. They often require the most time of any part of a statue because of the fine touch required to apply minute brush strokes—

remember there is no blending of color even in the pupils of the eyes.

Once the statue was completely painted, I sprayed on layer after layer of Ultra Glaze to give the work a porcelain-like finish, protect the paint, and preserve the colors from fading. It took hours to dry. Pressed for time, I stayed up almost the entire Saturday night to retouch and apply the final strokes of paint to the statue—some even after the glaze had been applied.

I completed the Saint Joseph statue with less than an hour before I needed to load it in my car and drive it back in time for Mass. I know it was still wet as I can remember getting paint on myself, just positioning the statue in the back of my station wagon.

The statue was placed back on the altar just moments before Mass. I doubt that anyone in attendance even noticed the painstaking restoration in which I had engaged during that week-long marathon painting session, but it did not matter one bit. I was pleased to look upon it in its restored condition, from that point on, knowing that I had played a part in returning it to its former brilliance.

At the same time that my statue painting interest was growing, I managed to fish my way into the *Guinness Book of World Records*. It was a life-changing event that would lead me to run my own bass fishing tournament business for the next 10 years. As I said, sometimes, one passion will give way to another, and my statue painting was interrupted for more than two decades.

I have since returned to statue painting, although I find that my fine touch has not—most likely due to a significant decline in my eyesight. Still, I have found ways to compensate through the use of better brushes, improved lighting, magnifying glasses…and lots of patience.

And speaking of patience, no activity could have tested more of mine than bass fishing, as you will see in the next chapter.

'I often feel closest to God as I am painting.
I frequently pray for God to use my work
to bless the lives of those who see it.
To me, if people receive anything good
from these paintings, I have to believe
it came from God rather than me.'
—Thomas Kinkade

Chapter 14:
Better Living through Bass Fishing

*'Enjoy the little things, for one day
you may look back and realize
they were the big things.'*
—Robert Brault

Can one day change the course of your life? I am living proof that it can. On October 28, 1984, I caught bass number 3,001 in 77 days of fishing—landing me in the *Guinness Book of World Records* for the most fish caught in a season. So much of my life has been altered by that one event—which remains a current record. My confidence level soared. I overcame my fear of public speaking. I went on to design lures, star in bass fishing videos, write a freshwater column and feature articles, and start and run my own business, Dave Romeo Bass Fishing Tournaments, for 10 years.

What I gained most from this event was the belief that if you have faith in God, confidence in yourself, and you are willing to persevere, there is virtually nothing you cannot accomplish.

I also acquired a mentor and book contract on the very same day when editor of the Guinness Book and chairman of the board of Sterling Publishing, David Boehm, asked if I wanted to write a book on bass fishing, and in 1988, I published my first book *Better Bass Fishing—the Dave Romeo Way.*

Writing any book is always a thrill, but that first one was just something else. I could not believe it when I first held it in my hands. Many of my self-doubts and inadequacies were put to rest knowing that I had been published—that my words and ideas had meaning to others. It represented validation and recognition in my field which made it easier to attract national sponsors and endorsement contracts from fishing tackle companies. I could see that my bass fishing record was a vehicle for reaching unlimited levels of success—even in non-fishing related fields. It was at this point that I learned the art of promotion, writing contracts, and public speaking.

By the way, in 2007, I caught and released bass # 25,000. In the interest of time, I will encourage you to read *Striving for Significance* which, thoroughly documents this entire adventure—as well as the life lessons learned along the way.

Although the following anecdote does not involve bass fishing, I could not pass up the opportunity to share one of my greatest fishing memories with you, which happened in July of 2005, when I fished in Loch Ness, Scotland.

Since I was a boy, I dreamed of fishing in the waters of Loch Ness. It took many years to complete this task, which I detailed in my book *Stumbling Onto Success*. What I have not previously shared in writing was, in 2005, the year my wife and I took a European cruise to celebrate our 15th wedding anniversary, there were no cruise ships stopping at Inverness, Scotland. That meant that in order for me to fish Loch Ness, we needed to arrive in London, England three days before the cruise began. I could hop a bus to the tube station, take a train to Gatwick Airport, and from there, catch the one and only flight to Inverness, Scotland that day.

My travel agent located a fishing guide on Loch Ness who had a friend that worked as a cab driver. When I was done fishing (and shopping for souvenirs at the gift shop), the cab driver would pick me up at Inverness Airport to catch the one and only flight back to London that day, and repeat the train and bus trips in reverse order back to my hotel. If I missed any of my connections, my chances of accomplishing this goal would virtually drop to zero. I could hardly sleep the night before and I did not need an alarm clock to be ready to go—though I would not chance it without one.

As luck would have it, every step of the way went off without a hitch. The brook trout were biting and I was able to achieve my goal. All I can say is if you want something so strongly, I encourage you to pursue it with every ounce of energy you have. The rewards will be well worth the sacrifices.

When I hung up my fishing rod in 2007, I promised myself that I would not replace bass fishing with another endeavor requiring as much time away from my wife. As you will see in chapter 15, the next passion not only takes place exclusively in our home, but has become an activity Kim and I can pursue together.

> *'Passion is about moving beyond our obligation and on to those things we most love to do. When you focus on things you really like to do, you are likely to do them with passion—and do them remarkably well!'*
> —Mark Sanborn

Chapter 15:
Solving Our Puzzle Dilemma

*'What mighty contests rise
from trivial things.'*
—Alexander Pope

I remember many years ago asking my wife Kim if she wanted to do a jigsaw puzzle together. In fact, I believe I asked her several times before she reluctantly acquiesced. It was a big puzzle—1,000 pieces. I believe it took us a good four or five days to complete.

I was having the time of my life. It stimulated my mind. It challenged my decision-making and analytical skills, and it was so rewarding to be able to visually witness the accomplishment of this shared goal. We were having a great time working on the puzzle together...*or so I thought.*

It was probably about three days into our jigsaw puzzle project when Kim and I were driving back home from a restaurant. She shocked me by exclaiming, *'I can't wait until we are done with that stupid puzzle!'*

I could not believe what I was hearing! I naturally inquired why she did not enjoy doing the puzzle. It seems that Kim's expectations of doing the puzzle *'together'* were far different from mine. She continued, *'You don't say a word to me. You do all of the water, and buildings and the houses while I get stuck doing the sky. You will fixate on that puzzle every time you pass the dining room table and ignore your other chores, and you will stay up late working on it when I have to go to bed.'*

Not having done a jigsaw puzzle in many years, and certainly not since I had been married, I was still viewing the activity from my familiar male perspective. It was a *'shoulder to shoulder'* activity which men enjoy very much like watching a football game, duck hunting, or going fishing. Men will sit next to each other for hours during these activities—each deriving endless satisfaction by being in close proximity to one another—without requiring a lot of conversation to enjoy the shared experience.

Women, on the other hand love relationships. They crave connection—especially with their spouses. This primarily comes through *'face to face'* activities like dining out or catching up on the day's events. Obviously, understanding my wife's perspective was an aspect our relationship in which I still needed to improve—actually, one of many.

We made some adjustments. First I agreed not to work on the puzzle without Kim being there so it was truly a team activity. Second, I discovered that Kim *actually liked* doing puzzles, provided they did not take several days to complete. She preferred a puzzle that we could complete from start to finish in one day. As a result, we scaled back from the 1,000 piece puzzles, to the 300 and 500 piece varieties.

The next adjustment came from the way we approached the puzzle. We originally just pulled pieces out of the box that looked like something we needed. In retrospect, it is no wonder it took us so long to complete the puzzles. Now, we take all of the pieces out of the box up front. Kim loves to put together the border first and she is very good at it. I am good at finding the border pieces and putting them aside for my wife.

Kim looks at the cover of the puzzle box and then decides on which items she wishes to work. With that knowledge, I begin sorting the similar colored pieces; reds in one pile, white in another, the house in still another pile, so each of us can take the ones we will be working on and begin assembling the puzzle.

There is also more conversation now than before, although it is still a relatively quiet pursuit. There is a greater consciousness of what the other person is working on, and an awareness of each other's needs. We experience a feeling of synergy as each of us drops our respective portions into the assembled frame, and we see the pieces come together as a whole.

Not only has this system made puzzling more enjoyable for both of us, but we also discovered that we could routinely complete a 500-piece puzzle in just under three hours, and a 300-piece puzzle in about 90 minutes.

Our jigsaw puzzle dilemma proved to be a very valuable learning experience on finding the proper balance for both of us to enjoy the same activity. It is amazing what we discover about ourselves through such simple diversions. The most rewarding validation I have discovered through our revisions is now Kim proactively asks me if I want to do a puzzle.

One of my favorite quotes by Arthur Conan Doyle goes, *'Once you eliminate the impossible, whatever remains, no matter how improbable, must be the truth.'* This is most obvious to me when working on a puzzle.

When I am trying to locate a missing piece of the puzzle, I visually scan the remaining loose pieces, and select what I think is the most likely one. More often than not, I have guessed wrong and discover that it is not the right piece. Starting with the most obvious selection, each time I will continue trying to fit a remaining piece back into the corresponding space, until I find the matching piece. It is amazing how many times I can look at a piece and be convinced that I have the correct one, only to discover that I am wrong.

When I have used up all but the seemingly least likely piece, and have no other options to select from, I discover that the remaining puzzle piece is in fact the correct one. How often do we jump to wrong conclusions about why people do what they do, only because we do not have all of the pieces of information we need to know the truth?

What I have learned from my puzzle passion is that you can use your best judgment, but that does not mean you will always be correct. When you guess wrong, do not be discouraged. You are learning. Use all available data, and the process of elimination to make wise decisions, and eventually you too will see things begin to fall into place.

'By the mile, it's a trial. By the yard, it's hard, but by the inch, everything's a cinch.'
—Old adage

Chapter 16:
The Joy of Writing

*'If you would not be forgotten, as
soon as you are dead and rotten,
either write things worth reading,
or do things worth the writing.'*
—*Benjamin Franklin*

Mother Teresa once described herself as, *'a little pencil
in the hand of a writing God who is sending a love letter
to the world.'* Now contrast her comment with that of
American writer and poet, Dorothy Parker, who said, *'I
hate writing. I love having written.'* While I do not hate
writing, I do appreciate what she meant. Writing is like
exercise—it is a means to achieving an end. Most of us
do not exercise because we love getting winded, sweating
profusely, and smelling like a fitness club locker room.
We exercise in spite of these things. We want instead what
we will gain by exercising; fitness, strength, agility, good
health, and a more attractive appearance. We want the
end. We want the results.

It is difficult to adequately explain the feeling that comes over me between the time I have completed the writing of a book, and the time it is actually published, but it is the only time when I actually fear dying. With all the thought, time, and preparation that have gone into completing a book, there is just no peace for an author until you actually hold a published copy of your work in your hands, knowing that others may now do the same.

Writing allows you the opportunity and privilege to reach another soul whom you may never otherwise even see. Like the other passions, it is also a connection. The genius of Jane Austen is the gift she had for painting people, like Elizabeth Bennett in *Pride and Prejudice,* or Elinor Dashwood in *Sense and Sensibility,* with such identifiably likeable qualities that, nearly a century after her death in 1817, her classic romantic novels can go on moving and inspiring readers with her gift for words and her portraits of human nature.

I get lost in Charles Dickens novel *The Life and Adventures of Nicholas Nickelby,* which describes in minute detail the personalities common to 19th century London and the surrounding areas. I find it amusing that Dickens wrote—after the novel's publication, and despite it being a work of fiction—that several Yorkshire schoolmasters threatened to sue him for slandering their establishments when describing the horrible conditions and treatments of the boarding school boys, at *Dotheboy's Hall.* He truly paints the most vivid caricatures of the people, places, and culture of the time. And how ironic it is to see, how little we have changed in our ways since 1839.

Having never had a sister, I was captivated by the relationships of the four March sisters in Louisa May Alcott's classic novel, *Little Women*. What a masterpiece! I was so fascinated to see her explore the complicated and multifaceted dynamics of six women all living under the same roof during Civil War times in Concord, Massachusetts. Alcott once declared she did not think she could write a successful book for girls and, like Dorothy Parker, did not enjoy writing one. She confessed in her diary, *'I plod away, although I don't enjoy this sort of things.'*

I was not a big fan of the formal education I received, and I could not wait to be done with college. I had more credits in English and I realized I could most quickly graduate as an English major, which I did in 1981, from Adelphi University in Garden City, New York. It seemed as good a major as any; after all, I could use it in so many fields.

I originally thought I would become an English teacher at that college. When I mentioned my plan to the dean of the English department, he replied, *'We'd love to have you, but they will have to carry one of us out of here feet first before we have an opening.'*

Since that did not pan out, I took a job as a bank teller, then as a tax consultant, a recruiter for the printing industry, and then as a results coach, and a motivational speaker. It took me 18 years to really use my major thoroughly in an occupation, yet it has always played a significant role in my success. Thirty-one years later, I have used my love of writing to compose countless poems and songs, 66 seminar lesson plans (so far) and publish nine books, not including this one. While I do truly enjoy writing in all of these forms, it is as an author to which I refer when I think of writing as my passion.

Writing is also discipline. The obligation to the reader to take him or her to a place from which he or she cannot return without you is paramount. *They must see through your words.* Just as Ann Sullivan would describe every word, occurrence, and nuance to Helen Keller by spelling out finger signals at about 80 words per minute in the palm of her hand, you, as the writer, take on a responsibility to show the reader what you envision in your mind.

One of the most fascinating aspects of writing is that you never really know at the outset where you are going to find yourself. Just adding the slightest reference to colorize your work can take hours or even days to research its true usage, and make sure your meaning will be understood. Often, I will make a statement that I am certain will be challenged by an editor, and yet it passes through without the slightest mention, while one of the proofreaders will stop me in my tracks about a casual phrase I cannot even remember including.

One time I used the expression *'flesh out'* as in, *'I want to flesh out an idea more thoroughly.'* My father, who did a lot of my pre-publication read-throughs balked at the term—he had never heard it used before and did not understand its meaning. That lead to me repeatedly stopping and asking every person I could locate if they understood that term, to see if it should stay in the manuscript, or be ousted because of its obscurity.

In one of my books, I was referring to a gentle precipitation—too light to be classified as a rain shower. I wanted to use the word *'spritz'* to describe the occurrence (this was before you could instantly look up anything under the sun on the internet). Try as I did, I could not find the spelling for this word anywhere. I finally settled on the term *'sun sprinkle',* although in my mind it was always a glaring place holder for the true description.

One could almost compare writing to hiking. As you embark, you have some idea of where you want to go, and what you might encounter along the way, yet quite often there are many unplanned diversions and rabbit trails down which an author winds up pursuing. You may occasionally get lost for a time, and have to work your way back to your intended trail towards familiarity.

Writing is therapy; you gain a peace when you truly capture your innermost thoughts in words—frequently leading to self-discovery and deeper insights into your true feelings. A great deal of problem solving occurs through the writing process. Often, after writing about a dilemma to express to a pen pal, I would see the solution to the problem which had previously eluded me.

Writing can be a cathartic experience if you are delving into a personally painful event. It is a feeling of spiritual release and purification brought about by an intensely emotional process. There is always a lesson to be learned, and the act of writing allows you to explore and discover that lesson and make peace with yourself.

Writing is a willingness to be vulnerable. It is a sharing of one's most private thoughts, feelings, and emotions for all to see. Once you are published, there is no going back. As I often say to my job coaching clients, when it comes to the importance of making a positive first impression, remember *you can't unpaint a house.* And, once published, *you also can't unwrite a book.* After you have done it, you cannot undo it. I must admit that it is sometimes unnerving when someone you hardly know comes up to you and starts talking about a personal aspect of your life which you have not told him or her, and you realize it was in one of your books.

Years ago, my father was reading through a pre-published version of my *Stumbling Onto Success* manuscript and he commented, *'You really put yourself out there.'* I said, *'I know, but when I tell these stories, these are the things people tell me helped them the most in their own lives.'* It is a risk to expose oneself in writing to the scrutiny of the world, but like art, writing is not done solely for the benefit of the public but is a form of expression for the author. I do not write to please the world but to make the world a more pleasing place. Still, I truly believe that one does not earn the right to be called an author merely by writing, but rather by being worthy of the reader's time.

> **'An artist has a duty to follow his muse—even when it leads him down an unexpected or inconvenient path.'**
> **—Thomas Kinkade**

Chapter 17:
Charlie's Challenge

'Alone we can do so little;
together we can do so much.'
—Helen Keller

Just as some of your own passions will overlap with one another, occasionally you may find that someone else's passion may lead you to discover one of your own. That was the case with me on August 7, 2009—my 50th birthday. Ironically it fell on a Thursday, which meant I would be presenting a seminar. The event had taken on a life of its own. What started out being just another seminar for 20 to 25 customers, had sprawled into a spectacular crowd of 51 people coming from all different states to celebrate my special day with me. The seminar had become almost an incidental formality, but the feeling was electrifying.

One of my long-time clients and friends, Leon Miller, called me about a month before with a proposition. He wanted to give me a $50.00 bill for my birthday, with a condition—I had to find a way to multiply the $50.00 and use it for a good purpose. Since I am continuously giving my clients challenges, I could not refuse this one from Leon, but I must admit, I was stumped. The $50.00 bill sat on my bureau for months. I did not know what to do with it. How was I supposed to turn that $50.00 into something significant?

In September, I received an E-mail from one of my Hall of Fame clients Charlie Mann. Charlie worked at Harley-Davidson Motor Company. His E-mail stated that 10 years earlier, Charlie was diagnosed with Lymphoma. He recalled how when he first learned of his medical condition, he wondered if he would ever live to see his daughter, Alexa, get married. A decade later, after many humbling experiences, painful treatments, and a devotion to his faith, Charlie is cancer free.

Charlie attached a photo of him dancing the '*father of the bride dance*' with his lovely daughter. I could not get that image out of my mind. The joy, the sheer happiness in their expressions capturing that special moment in time—it was a milestone for the entire family. One would have to be made of stone not to be moved by that priceless image.

In gratitude to the Leukemia and Lymphoma Society for helping him return to health, Charlie decided he was going to run a marathon for the organization. His goal was to raise $10,000—$1,000 for each year he has been cancer-free.

About that same time, the very first *Leadership Academy* was about to begin. This is a special five-week program to develop real-world leadership skills in the participants. One of the requirements of this program was that the participants take on a class project. Leon Miller was also part of this class and offered a challenge—that the *Leadership Academy* help Charlie Mann raise half of the money needed for his cause. Since Charlie, who was not a member of the class but was well-known and well-liked by virtually the entire class, the participants decided to organize *Charlie's Challenge*—an auction conducted as a fundraiser for the Leukemia and Lymphoma Society. I was not sure how it would turn out but, at least now I had a place to donate Leon's $50.00 bill.

I invited Charlie Mann to attend the final *Leadership Academy* class so he could find out that the group had selected his charity as their class project. Charlie confided to me later that he was so humbled—originally believing I had asked him to address the graduation members because I viewed him as such an exceptional leader. When he learned of their decision to support him out of love and friendship, he broke down sobbing in front of the entire class. He was moved, as was I, that each of the participants requested having his or her individual photographs taken with our beneficiary.

Keeping in mind that most of the participants had never done anything like this before, it was remarkable to watch how in the span of just over three hours, that magical force of 11 people, supported by a team of volunteers, combined to generate more than $5,000 for *Charlie's Challenge.*

One individual, Kevin Fry, wound up raising more money for Charlie's cause than Harley-Davidson. Charlie not only met his $10,000 goal—he surpassed it. In fact, when Charlie went to California for his marathon, the Leukemia and Lymphoma Society had their top 10 fundraisers stand up. Imagine Charlie's surprise to learn he was number seven in the nation!

I still marvel how that two-month-old *Leadership Academy* could run a project so large that no single one of them could have handled on his or her own. It was amazing and gratifying to watch as each one did his or her part to execute a magnificent event for the benefit of all those involved. They were exhilarated knowing that they had each in their own way contributed and participated in the incredible process of making a dream come true. It would surely be a day that everyone involved will never forget and remember with a sense of pride, joy, and fulfillment.

It demonstrated the power of friendship, love, and purpose when focused like a laser beam on a worthy cause. It was indeed a passion worth pursuing. I can only imagine that it was one of Charlie Mann's top 20 best memories; and it also allowed me to indulge in a number of my own passions, namely public speaking, coaching, and event planning.

> *'Never doubt that a small group of thoughtful, committed citizens can change the world; indeed, it's the only thing that ever has.'*
> *—Margaret Mead*

Chapter 18:
Cruising

'Success will not come easy, and if it does, it's not really success. Success exacts a price, but it also delivers a prize. There will always be an exchange of effort for reward.'
—*John Maxwell*

When we first got married, Kim suggested that we save up for a cruise. She knew I was not a big fan of the beach and she thought that this might be more to my liking. Prior to this, I had never really thought about taking a cruise, but Kim had cruised to Bermuda with two of her girlfriends before we met. She spoke of how much she loved the experience. I agreed it sounded like a great time. We saved up for five years, and made our first cruise to Alaska in 1995 to celebrate our fifth wedding anniversary.

We selected the inside passage cruise because Kim had a strong fascination with the 49th state, and because we thought it would be more comfortable in a cool environment as opposed to a tropical one.

It was incredible sailing through Glacier Bay National Park, seeing 13 bald eagles sitting together feeding at low tide, spying Mount McKinley—the highest mountain in North America, and fishing in the salmon capital of the world, Ketchikan. What was even more enjoyable was '*the cruise ship experience.*' If you have never been on a cruise ship, please allow me to explain.

All of our cruises have been with Princess Cruises. We have never been disappointed with their service. In fact, Princess Cruises is one of the companies I use as an example of outstanding service leaders in my seminar entitled, *In Search of Legendary Customer Service.*

For someone who is a coach by profession, cruising is the perfect environment to study how serious companies demonstrate their mastery for treating guests. Granted, the food in the restaurants on the cruise ship is excellent, but you can find that just about anywhere. What is different is the service. Nightly, 500 people are seated for dinner within three minutes of the doors opening. I defy you to find a landside restaurant anywhere that can pull off this feat.

There is a head waiter and an assistant waiter assigned to each table. On that first cruise, Giorgio, our assistant waiter, was a young man from Italy who had not yet mastered the English language. I remember asking him at our first meal for some more brown sugar packets as I used up all the ones on our table in my unsweetened iced tea. From that point on, and without ever saying another word, our table was decked out with a second sweetener holder—stocked *exclusively* with brown sugar packets—without fail at every meal for the rest of our cruise. This man understood what it means to satisfy even the unexpressed needs of customers. We experienced legendary customer service on every cruise from London to Hawaii, and even back again to Alaska, and from every department of Princess Cruises, both on and off the ship.

These people live to serve their guests, and we love it. Like our cabin steward in the South Pacific who made sure every time we left our cabin that he would empty our trash and restock our refrigerator. They are passionate about excelling in the little things, like placing chocolate mints on the pillows every evening. Kim and I are passionate about noticing and appreciating the little things.

There are so many simple joys that come from taking a two-week escape from work and worry to relax and enjoy the pure pleasure afforded to passengers on a cruise ship. Here are just a few examples:

I gave the piano player in the ship's lounge $5.00 once after he successfully accepted my challenge to segue from *Phantom of the Opera's Music of the Night* into the tropical island standard *Yellow Bird*. Each tiny treasured instance almost takes on a life of its own.

Kim and I entered our stateroom after breakfast one morning while cruising through the inside passage of Alaska, and witnessed through our over-sized cabin window, a humpback whale breaching out of the water.

We were thrilled when we won Princess Cruise baseball caps by taking first place in the ship's *Seinfeld* Trivia contest. It is the unequalled, stress-free enjoyment that comes from having the ability to take an afternoon hot tub break as you enjoy reading a good book while passing by the white cliffs of Dover, followed by a bratwurst snack before dinner.

We enjoyed meeting people from all over the world who add color to our lives with their fascinating backgrounds, and discovering those unique coincidences that we have in common.

And, those unforgettable souvenirs that become a part of our life, like my Tahitian ruler which I use every week as I send out seminar information to my clients, or the soft, cotton handkerchiefs I picked up in Dublin, Ireland after not packing enough for our European cruise. It is also the magnificent framed photograph in our family room of a mother moose feeding in a lake at the foot of Mount McKinley, which we found while staying at the Princess Lodge in Denali National Park. I was stunned to learn that the park is larger than the State of Massachusetts.

I must include a final memory from our 10th wedding anniversary. In 2000, Kim and I took a cruise of the South Pacific. Starting in Tahiti, we sailed to Moorea, Bora Bora, Christmas Island, Kauai, Maui, Oahu, and the big island of Hawaii. It was indeed the cruise of a lifetime. (Please read my book *Stumbling Onto Success* for an even more detailed description of some of our Hawaiian highlights.)

One moment, not previously shared in my books, is of the day we spent in Bora Bora—rightfully called *the most beautiful island in the world.* The atoll itself is such a spectacular array of emerald green mounts surrounded by vibrant turquoise and sky blue colors. It is indeed how many people would envision paradise.

After spending the day on the island, Kim and I were preparing to go to dinner aboard the Princess Cruise ship. I had been secretly saving up for a year to give Kim a 10th wedding anniversary band. I walked her to our cabin window overlooking the magnificent orange sun about to set over Bora Bora. I said, *'I want to create a memory. Look at the island. Now look at my face.'* I repeated those instructions to Kim two more times and then, I slipped the ring onto her finger. It was just one of those perfect moments in time that you happily keep with you for the rest of your life.

There is such an overpowering feeling of joy that comes from the shared memories, the photo albums, and the enduring friendships one picks up while traveling the world by water in the lap of luxury. It is a temporary escape from reality, and a glimpse as to how nice this world can be sometimes.

> **'Your time on this earth is brief.**
> **Consider the days, and be wise.'**
> **—Thomas Kinkade**

Chapter 19:
Love and Marriage

'What's loved is never lost.'
—Small Miracles of Love and Friendship

The very first time I presented my seminar entitled *Designing Your Destiny,* one of my Hall of Fame clients, Art Noel, asked me if your marriage could be your passion. I must admit, I did not have a good answer for him at that time, but that was in 2002. I have since come to see the wisdom in Art's question, and now I do believe that your marriage and your family not only *can be* but *should be* your passion.

I thought back to how this relates to my own situation and our wedding day. Since most of my family was from Long Island, New York and most of Kim's family was from Lancaster, Pennsylvania, we faced a perplexing logistical dilemma—where should we get married?

While there was no question in my mind that I wanted to get married in my church, we knew that a New York wedding reception could be pretty expensive, and we did not want to start off our marriage by incurring massive amounts of debt. This became prophetic later on, as I lost my job just six weeks before our wedding. In addition, we knew some of Kim's family might not be able to make the journey to New York so we came up with a unique solution. We got married at Saint Pius V Chapel in Oyster Bay Cove on Long Island at 6:00 PM on February 23, 1990. It was dark and cold, but so many of our friends and family were there to witness our ceremony, and add their warmth. We went to dinner that Friday night at a small Italian restaurant.

The next morning, we got in our cars and drove four hours from Long Island to Central Pennsylvania where our wedding reception took place at the Eden Resort in Lancaster County, on Saturday at 6:00 PM.

It was my first encounter with the Eden Resort, which has now become *'home ice'* to Dave Romeo Seminars. As of this writing, I have presented over 185 seminars at the Eden Resort—the finest and most guest-focused organization with whom I have ever worked. They came to our rescue several times during our reception, and set the bar exceedingly high for any place at which I have presented seminars after that, and I will always be grateful to them for doing so.

The reception was beautiful, with so many loved ones gathered together to share in our joyous celebration. Once again, my two best friends, Peter and Artie, were there at my side along with relatives from both the Romeo and Trout sides of the family.

Throughout our marriage, I discovered what a truly remarkable woman I had married. I never knew someone could love me so much, but Kim humbles me with her goodness and expressions of thoughtfulness.

One specific demonstration of her love occurred in 1998. Unbeknownst to me at the time, Kim had planned an elaborate surprise birthday party for my 40th birthday. It fell on a Thursday that year, so the date was set for Saturday, August 9. Since we usually celebrated my birthday with another one of my fishing buddies, Mike, and his wife, Patti (whose birthday was August 10), I was not the least bit suspicious even when Kim suggested that Mike and I go fishing that day, and then meet her and Patti at a local restaurant at 5:00 PM. Kim figured that Mike—who was in on the surprise—would make sure I stayed away long enough for Kim to get everything in place. What she did not plan on was that Mike forgot to wear *his watch* that day, and *my watch* had stopped working the day before.

We fished the Susquehanna River for hours, enjoying the hot sunny day, not giving much concern to the time. On the way back in, we encountered a muddy sandbar which made getting back to the boat launch ramp more difficult—and more time consuming.

When we finally made it back to shore and got Mike's boat back on the trailer, we looked at the time. It was about 4:45 PM. We were about 20 minutes away from home and I had to unpack the car, shave, shower, get dressed, and get to the restaurant, which was about another 20 minutes away.

Pursuing Your Passions!

I will be the first to admit that when it comes to being married, I am not the fastest learner. Still, in eight years, one thing I did know was that Kim hates it when I make her late for something. This was not good. As Mike drove us to my house, I contemplated the best course of action. I said, *'Why don't I just go in and put on a clean set of clothes and skip the shower.'* Knowing what lie ahead for us, Mike quickly shot down my suggestion, instead using my brief shower pit stop as an opportunity to call the restaurant and let Kim know we were running late.

A few minutes after we left my house we were flying down the road, Mike sliding from side to side as I drove wildly toward the restaurant to meet my fate. When we arrived at the restaurant—whose staff were well aware of the surprise party—I approached the greeter and said, *'My name is Dave Romeo and I am looking for an angry, red-headed woman.'* He said, *'Right this way.'* Since Mike was in on the surprise, he dropped back from me to avoid the impending moment of truth.

I was so worried about Kim's reaction that I was completely oblivious that the greeter was leading us through the restaurant and into the back room. Once inside I was searching for Kim, when my eye caught the glance of one of my clients. I thought to myself, *'Oh there's Jeff. I have to remember to go over and say hello to him later after Kim kills me.'* I went a few more feet, and saw my best friend, Peter Nicholson, standing next to my parents, and their neighbors from East Meadow, NY, John and Sonia Karpowich, and all of them were smiling. All of

123

a sudden, it finally dawned on me that it was a surprise party—*in my honor!*

The juxtaposition of family, friends, clients, past employers, and neighbors was overwhelming. It really endeared Kim to me even more so after that event because she had done such a magical job of pulling it off without me catching on. All I had to do was drink it in and enjoy it.

My marriage and my time with Kim has become an intense passion of happiness and love. It grows stronger by the day. She is my greatest earthly gift. Even when there are disagreements, I see them as opportunities for me to grow by practicing humility and avoiding giving into my ego, so I can become a better man. I challenge you to improve your relationship with your spouse and your children so you too can become a better person.

> **'Learn to find joy in the littlest things.'**
> **—Dave Romeo**

Chapter 20:
Friendship

'Passion comes from a commitment
born of doing what you love and doing
it for people who matter to you.'
—*Mark Sanborn*

Can friendship be a passion? Of course it can! What would life be like without having people with whom to share your happy memories?

Ask anyone who has been to my seminars what day of the week they are on and they will tell you, *'That's easy. They are on Thursdays.'* I share this with you to impress upon you that I had no divine plan to make sure that my 50th birthday fell on the day of a seminar. No biggie. I do not mind spending my birthday presenting a seminar. In fact, I love spending the day with my clients. I truly enjoy their company. However, I imagine that a 50th birthday is just one of those milestones in the life of anyone who hits that number.

When I was preparing the 2008 seminar schedule the year before (probably in April 2007) I asked one of my coworkers if she thought I should mention that I would be doing a seminar on my 50th birthday, she said, *'Sure, why not?'*

With that validation, I listed the August 7, 2008 seminar as *How to Make a Perfect First Impression (Dave Romeo's 50th Birthday Bash)*. I did not think it would make much of a difference as far as people signing up, but I also figured it would not keep anyone away either. *I was way off!* Normally, I would expect that seminar to attract about 20 to 25 people. As the word spread, the seminar ended up with 51 attendees. Not only that, but it became the fourth highest-grossing seminar up until that time and still to this day, remains the single, highest-grossing seminar (not including Hall of Fame seminars).

But it was not just *how many* people were there. It was also *who* was there. My wife, Kim, was there. Also, my parents were there. They came to visit us in Pennsylvania, for the fifth and last time. It was the only time my parents ever heard me present a live seminar and meet my clients. Barbara Anglim—my dear friend of 30 years—drove in from New Jersey. There is just something about seeing so many of your favorite people all together in the same room. In fact, eight of my current top 10 all-time seminar attendees were present, including Bob Kandratavich, who has been with me since my very first seminar in January 1999, and my number one all-time customer, Elaine Bledsoe, who has attended every one of my 66 seminars. The seminar itself was great and well-received. The people were just pouring out their love, and it was a memory I will cherish for the rest of my life.

I could not imagine a chapter about friendship without telling you about the most recent memory on my top 20 list. A lot of time has passed since the first day of eighth grade, but in 1971, I met my two best friends, Art Gardner and Peter Nicholson, whom I have been telling you about throughout this book. On November 19, 2011, the three of us reunited in Hollywood, Florida to celebrate 40 years of friendship. We have been through so many situations together. Their past is my past. Their history is my history—and I would not have it any other way!

Because of distance (Artie lives in Florida and Peter lives in New York), we do not get together as often as we would like, but we have made it a point to get together every five years. And when we do, it is as if we have never been apart.

There is a magic that descends on the three of us when we get together. Whatever adolescent memory two of us may have forgotten—*whether intentionally or unintentionally*—the third is sure to retain and regale. I never laugh as much in a year's time as I do when I am in the company of my two best friends. One time, Artie's son was watching the three of us reminiscing and cracking up over some youthful recollection. He observed, *'You guys are like kids in grown-up bodies.'*

I must admit there are times when I am alone that I will catch myself laughing uncontrollably, because I start remembering one of our high school memories; and perhaps, that is what binds us through more than 40 years of friendship. It has also been 40 years of laughter. How can you not love two people who have contributed so much fun, joy, and camaraderie to your earthly existence?

I realize that not everyone gets two life-long friends to share your ups and downs with through five decades and I do not take this for granted. It more than makes up for some of the more difficult moments one encounters through a lifetime. It is a privilege I would not trade for all the tea in China.

Another great memory demonstrates that different passions often combine to create spectacular highpoints you will never forget. In this particular case, we are talking about the combination of great friends and peacock bass fishing. *What could be better than that?*

In the *Stumbling Onto Success* book, I wrote about my first attempt to catch a peacock bass in 2000 while fishing on the island of Oahu. And while my first endeavor fell short, I never stopped thinking about the day when I would once again get another opportunity to land one of those colorful fish.

After that book's release, Art Gardner read of my interest and promised me that the next time I came to visit him in southern Florida, he would arrange to take me peacock bass fishing with him. In 2009, he made good on his word.

Artie secured a small boat with an electronic motor from some friends who really did not fish, but lived on a small pond of a few acres in Pembroke Pines, Florida. *Perfect!* This is exactly the type of pond I enjoy fishing. Best of all, Artie confirmed in advance that the pond contained peacock bass.

Peacock bass, which are native to the Amazon River basin, were originally introduced into the waters of southern Florida in 1984, in an attempt to control the growing population of non-native species of fish, including oscars. The peacock bass have now made their way into virtually all of the waterways in the southern part of the Sunshine State.

Unlike my first excursion in Hawaii, this time we spotted several peacock bass almost immediately upon putting the boat in the water. However, *spotting them* was one thing—*catching them* was another.

Try as I did, all I could do was get these fish to swim away from my lures. We circled the entire pond, each catching several largemouth bass along the way. More valuable to me though than the mediocre fishing results was that special bonding time that comes when two close friends are alone in nature to reconnect by sharing the major (or even minor) events that have made an impact on them since last they saw each other. For Artie and I, it had been two years since we last got together, and much longer since we were completely by ourselves without anyone else, even our wives, to intrude on that time-tested and treasured bond of friendship.

We did not see any other peacock bass that morning except for the few we spotted when we first put in. It was now nearly five hours later, and we were fighting the clock because we had plans to meet with Fred and Irene Myers for lunch. Both of them were my clients who had moved away years earlier. In fact, Fred was one of the first two people inducted into Dave Romeo Seminars Hall of Fame in 2001. I was looking forward to seeing the Myers again nearly as much as I had been anticipating this peacock bass fishing trip with Artie.

Before we packed it in, I asked Artie to make another pass back to where we had first encountered the nesting peacock bass. This time, I broke all the rules. I had been told peacock bass only hit surface lures with treble hooks. Apparently, these fish did not get that message. I put on a small motor oil-colored plastic worm with a fluorescent orange flip tail on a single hook. After about 50 attempts to land a peacock bass, which repeatedly charged my lure, I set the hook and pulled in an incredible orange, black, and white butterfly peacock bass.

While I naturally wanted to take a few long-awaited pictures with this elusive striped gamefish, what I really wanted was a picture of Artie holding the fish visualizing, even back then, that it would one day be immortalized on the cover of this book. My best friend and a peacock bass, which he promised to help me catch—captured together on that beautiful November day in 2009. It was just another wonderful memory to cherish—the combination of two passions, friendship and fishing...

both all too rare, long-anticipated, and in the end, worth every second of the wait.

> *'One of the surest ways to build confidence is to find one thing you're good at and then specialize until you are special. It could be a sport, a task, a natural ability, or a personally developed talent.'*
> —*John Maxwell*

Chapter 21:
Coaching is a Passion for People

'Pain is the fuel of passion—it
energizes us with an intensity to change
that we don't normally possess.'
—Rick Warren

'Well, I am going to finally succumb to the system. I have
been getting praised and scrutinized for over-performing.
I'm just going to do the job as it is presented and do the best
as I can and no longer follow up with customers. I have been
told that me calling a customer back is an unfair advantage
so I will not buck what they are saying. I am the sum of all
my decisions – and I always try to go outside of the norm
which always gets me in trouble – so I won't do it this time
around.'

When I saw the above E-mail, which was sent to me
by one of my protégés of nine years, writing this discour-
aging message, several thoughts went through my mind.
First, how would you feel if you intercepted this E-mail

from an employee who had only been working for your bank for less than 90 days? Imagine if you saw how your bureaucratic practices were draining every last ounce of enthusiasm and ambition out of this man's body. What would you do to fix it?

As a coach, my role is to hold people accountable to achieving their dreams. I get them focused, offer clear directions and strategies, teach them to track their results, build them up when they suffer setbacks, and cheer them on when they succeed.

Employers like the one referenced in this chapter's opening E-mail are one of the reasons I have been a results coach since 1998. People need encouragement when they are scared, starting a new job or business, or going through a rough time.

It astounds me how many people—especially those employed in multi-level-marketing businesses—hire me to coach them even though they report to someone in that organization, whose job it is in part, to do the very same thing *for free!* What seems to be missing from the role of some supervisors, managers, uplinks, team leaders, and directors is the impact of support, encouragement, and inspiration on those employees, or associates who look up to them for their professional nourishment.

The act of coaching is a sacred sharing of (usually) two people—one seeking knowledge, wisdom, advice, and direction from the other, who is charged with the responsibility to deliver those results. It is a charge I take as seriously as my own reputation; after all, they are one and the same.

As I mentioned earlier, for years I have observed that the two most powerful messages that I impress upon my beloved coaching clients are *'I believe in you, and I am rooting for you.'* It is all too clear to me what a profound impact my mentors and coaches have had on my life, and I strive never to lose sight of just how much responsibility has been entrusted to me when I make the commitment to serve as someone's coach or mentor.

The true reward for coaching is not a monetary one, but rather the joy of seeing your clients fulfill their potential and deliver on their promise. When someone realizes just how amazing he or she really is for the very first time—perhaps in his or her life—you see that person blossom like a spring flower seeking the sun. I challenge you to let this chapter's initial E-mail serve as a wakeup call to you and your organization to lift the spirits of the people you employ, and inspire them to passionately and enthusiastically serve your customers.

> **'We fail not because of big problems,**
> **but because of small purposes.'**
> **—John Maxwell**

Part III:
Profiting from
Your Passions

Chapter 22:
Turn Your Passion into Your Profession

'Follow your passion. Find your place.'
—Ad for Missouri State University

In a perfect world, you can transform your passion into your profession. Every time I have the privilege to stand in front of an audience, sharing ideas, concepts, lessons, and stories (as I have for you throughout this book) and conclude to a round of applause from people who truly value their ability to grow personally, professionally, and spiritually, I am overcome with joy. Having long ago established my purpose—to do as much good as I possibly can, for as many people as I can possibly touch—I use this as my barometer for making sure I stay true to my values. You, too, can do the same.

My work has become an expression of who I am and what I believe. You can autograph your work with excellence, and show the world what you are capable of achieving through your good works and your passions. They will be the mile-markers of your success.

One of the many highlights of presenting seminars was the 10th Dave Romeo Seminars Hall of Fame Awards. Let me explain why.

At the very last seminar of the year, I announce the two newest Dave Romeo Seminar Hall of Fame winners. These are the people who—through any combination of coaching and/or seminars—have learned what they needed to be successful, applied the training, and achieved the most outstanding results.

Without a doubt, the Hall of Fame seminar is my favorite day of the year. Hardly a day goes by that I am not thinking about who will be the next two inductees to receive this honor. These selections are very personal to me, and represent the best of the best.

The Hall of Fame seminar is also the biggest and best attended seminar of the year, and traditionally breaks all the records each year for my single, highest-grossing speaking engagement. As I alluded to in the opening paragraph of this book's prologue, I pride myself on my reputation so people will know how highly I prize my Hall of Fame inductees.

An inductee cannot be eligible unless he or she is registered for the Hall of Fame seminar. I always select the most popular new seminar of the year, so it is new to everyone, and what I appreciate the most is that nearly every previous Hall of Famer makes a point to attend this seminar to see who will be the newest inductees.

No one—not the Hall of Famers, not the inductees, *not even my wife*—knows who will be named to the Hall of Fame until they are in the room, and I start describing the accomplishments that earned the inductees their honored place alongside the previous winners.

The 10th Dave Romeo Seminars Hall of Fame Awards Ceremony in 2010 was extra special. It was attended by 16 of the 20 Hall of Fame inductees, including Dwight Smith, who flew in from Florida to attend, having moved away three years earlier; and Art Noel, who had not been to a Hall of Fame event since his own induction in 2002. Some of these people had never even met before, and it was the greatest number of Hall of Famers ever assembled in one place at the same time.

As always, the air was electric, and the collection of so many of my favorite clients and friends (I have never really understood how to separate the two) all treating each other like members at their own annual family reunion was one of the most rewarding experiences of my life.

Many people I meet feel unfulfilled in their jobs. Often, they comment about how they wish they can do what they really love instead of what they have to do in order to make a living. I challenge them—and you— to do both. One of my mentors, Charlie 'Tremendous' Jones said, *'Don't wish for a better job. Do a better job, and you'll have a better job.'* Through your passions, you can make this world a worthwhile place to live and explore your talents and gifts. Once you have clearly identified your purpose, use your passions, and your occupation, to express them to others.

If you love art, and you work as a graphic artist, then you are probably already doing this, but if you work as a bank teller or a hardware store manager, be sure to take every opportunity of displaying your talents whenever the opportunities arise in your work. If they are not readily noticeable, then look more closely, or create them yourself. Do not deny yourself, or the world, access to your God-given talents.

Convert your calling to transform your job into your joy. Make your vocation your vehicle for displaying your gifts. There is hardly a moment that goes by in your day when you cannot inspire others by going above and beyond to please someone. Never underestimate the power of a smile when serving others, even in the most menial tasks. Come to recognize that each day will bring with it another set of circumstances and opportunities to graciously serve others.

> *'Your success in life will be in direct proportion to what you do after you do what you are expected to do.'*
> *—Brian Tracy*

Chapter 23:
A Passion for The Passion

*'Faith is like a muscle—the more you
exercise it, the stronger it becomes.'*
—Sandy Shaw

Up until now, we have looked at earthly passions, but let
us also explore a much more meaningful dimension—
prayer. It is an activity that has aided me in my life's
journey. While many people today tend to abandon their
faith in their adult lives, I can see how much stronger
my faith has grown through the years due in great part
from what I experienced through my dad.

I saw in my father a man who became more and more
immersed in his faith the longer he lived. This was most
noticeable in his prayer life. He set up a desk in his study,
and used his antiquated computer to type up specific
prayers that he liked, and repeated them often. He spent
more than an hour in his daily prayers, and never tired
of sharing passages that caught his interest with anyone
he saw. He even went so far as to become a Benedictine

oblate—the highest level a married man can achieve in the Catholic Faith—taking the name of Brother Henry.

What I admired most about my father is that he became a man who *lived* his faith, both inwardly and outwardly. It was rare to see him in his later years when he did not have a crucifix hanging from his neck, as you can see in his photograph on the cover of this book.

He was not afraid to challenge someone if they were misinformed about the Catholic Faith, yet he was always respectful and firm—and smiling that unmistakable '*Sal smile.*' (Although his name was Salvatore, I never heard anyone call him that. His friends called him Sal, but his family called him Ted and no one seems to know why.) It is funny that whether someone embraced his or her religion or not, my father always spoke to that person as if he or she should, and yet I never saw anyone react to him in any way other than with respect for this man who personified his religious beliefs.

It was so helpful to me to have a role model who not only inspired me to stand up for my convictions, but who helped my wife grow in her faith. Ironically, many of the things I learned about my religion came from Kim, who learned them from my father.

My father did not do things because *he had to*. He did things because *he wanted to*. He got his masters degree after retiring from the New York City police force, and he got his PhD in criminology at the age of 60—shortly before retiring from a career in banking. He was very proud of these accomplishments and displayed his diplomas in his study. Yet, it was clear from the items in that room, that the temporal accomplishments took a distant back seat to the matters of his Catholic faith.

One of the biggest challenges for someone trying to live a holy life today is to *'live in the world, but not of it.'* But that is what my father did. He walked the talk. His religion was his passion. His prayer life became the center of his day. It overshadowed almost every other aspect of his life, with his love of family, food, and bowling coming in a distant second, third, and fourth, respectively.

My dad was not a perfect man. Indeed, my mother told me, *'Everyone else would say how smart and helpful he was to them. To me—he was a pest.'* It is very easy for me to identify with that assessment. I am sure my wife would (and has) said the same thing about me. There is an old saying that goes, *'How long a minute is, depends on which side of the bathroom door you're standing.'* And maybe that is how it is when you give so much of yourself to others; you tend to shortchange those closest to you. It is impossible to be all things to all people so you must pick and choose how you will be seen.

I love him as much in heaven as I did when he was in Florida. To me, he does not seem any farther away now than he was before, and I look forward to the next time we see each other. He is with me every day, in lessons taught and remembered; in his laughter, and his mannerisms; and in his looks—which my wife often says she sees in my face when I smile at her.

It is truly amazing just how much impact a person can have on your life either by entering it or departing from it. Perhaps my father's most enduring legacy is what he taught me through his example: *Never give up when your cause is just.* I summoned my father's courage and dedication when I worked along with many others to open and establish Saints Peter & Paul Roman Catholic Mission.

From the time I moved to Pennsylvania in 1990 until we found a Traditional Catholic Church on January 25, 2004 was a nearly 14-year wait. It was an incredible accomplishment which became the basis for my book *Birth of a Chapel,* published in 2009. I encourage you to read that book for the full story, even though the celebration turned out to be short-lived but have no fear—in 2011, Saint Michael the Archangel Roman Catholic Church opened in Windsor, PA. With many of the same dedicated people and even more dedication to my father's memory (having lost him the year before), we persevered, and now enjoy the fruits of those challenging labors. Again, in the interest of time, I encourage you to read *Rebirth of a Chapel,* which chronicles the entire uplifting story. Please do not think I am skimping. On the contrary, these events were so monumental that they deserved their own complete texts.

When we are talking about passions, remember that there are the temporal kind and the eternal kind. Ultimately, it will be our passion for our faith that will determine our eternal rewards. It is never too soon to start focusing on them.

> **'If you want to live a happy life,**
> **seek to live a holy life'**
> **—John Maxwell**

Chapter 24:
The Haven

'Be it ever so humble, there's
no place like home.'
—John Howard Payne

I was recently speaking with Artie a few days after Christmas to check in and say hello. As we talked, I mentioned how much I now look forward to coming home from work. I used to try to squeeze in as much as I can at the end of the work day, short-changing Kim by getting home after her, even though I had a shorter commute time. Now, I cannot wait for 5 o'clock so I can get home.

Artie said he felt the same way, and that he loved to spend time at home. He could stay there for long periods of time and be content. I added that it really is true that your home is the most comfortable place in the world. I believe that most people feel the same way about their homes—big or small.

Artie agreed, and said, *'That is because your home is supposed to be a sanctuary; a haven where you can just enjoy your loved ones.'*

His comments stirred a long lost memory from over 30 years ago. Artie and I had something else in common. In 1977—the year after we graduated from high school and his family moved to south Florida—Artie stayed with my family for the entire summer. During that time, he was able to get a part-time job with me at Chicken Delight in Westbury, NY where I worked for five years while I completed my college education.

There was a repeat customer who ordered food from Chicken Delight about every couple of weeks or so. His name was Mr. Egan. He was probably in his late fifties or early sixties. His age showed mostly in his receding hairline and his gums. This was very noticeable because Mr. Egan always greeted me with a big smile every time I delivered his order—although I am sure he never knew my name. During those five years of employment, I delivered to hundreds of customers, and have forgotten most of them, but I will never forget Mr. Egan. Although his house was not very large or fancy, he had something that made it very distinctive. Hanging from the lamppost that I would pass on his walkway was a small black sign that simply read, *'The Haven.'*

I took note of that sign every time I delivered to the Egan residence. Finally, one day I asked Mr. Egan what the sign on his lamppost meant. He said, *'My wife and I just love our home and we think of it as a haven.'*

It was humble and modest, not particularly large—probably just the right size for a pair of empty-nesters—and yet to him and Mrs. Egan, it was the most comfortable place in the world. Not only that, but it only mattered to the two of them that they felt that way. Still, they were so happy about how they felt about their home, that they proudly displayed that sign out front for all to see. Wouldn't you love to have the Egans for your neighbors? These people understood that you never have to leave your home to experience your passion.

Our home is the place where many of our passions are housed, pursued, and enjoyed such as doing puzzles, keeping fit, viewing hockey games, bird-watching, listening to music, painting, praying, and obviously writing. I challenge you to make your home your haven. It will benefit you in every conceivable way.

'It truly is a wonderful life.'
—Jimmy Stewart
(as George Bailey in the movie, It's a Wonderful Life)

Conclusion:
Full Circle

'For everything you lose,
you gain something.'
—Dave Romeo

And so we have come full circle. Once more here are my top 20 most prized and treasured memories that have combined to create a thoroughly enjoyable and fulfilling life:

1. 2011 Celebrate 40 years of friendship with my two best friends

2. 2011 Saint Michael the Archangel Roman Catholic Church opens

3. 2010 The 10th Dave Romeo Seminars Hall of Fame Awards

4. 2009 Peacock bass fishing with Art Gardner in Florida

5. 2009 The Pittsburgh Penguins win the Stanley Cup

6. 2008 *The Big 5-0* 50th Birthday Bash seminar

7. 2007 Catching and Releasing Bass # 25,000 in 25 years

8. 2005 Fishing at Loch Ness, Scotland

9. 2004 Saints Peter & Paul Roman Catholic Mission opens

10. 2002 *Designing Your Destiny* is published

11. 2000 Bora Bora at sunset on our 10th Anniversary cruise

12. 1998 My 40th Birthday Surprise Party

13. 1990 Our Wedding Day

14. 1988 Publishing my first book *Better Bass Fishing—the Dave Romeo Way*

15. 1984 Established a Guinness World Record for bass fishing

16. 1981 The Rolling Stones at JFK Stadium in Philadelphia road trip

17. 1980 the New York Islanders win their first Stanley Cup Championship

18. 1978 Battle of the Bands victory

19. 1975 Seeing Led Zeppelin live in concert for the very first time

20. 1973 Soccer All-star game MVP

They mean even more to me now after sharing them with you because I want them to be an inspiration for you to do the same with your own favorite memories.

As I look back over my list with a greater time perspective on these events, it becomes clear that my focus has shifted from self-centeredness to more about others. I notice that the more people the memory includes, the more prized it has become. You may find that when all is said and done, what matters most to you are the cherished relationships that have lasted a lifetime.

You *are* the sum of your decisions. Decide wisely to consciously pursue your passions. What you will discover is that your passions stop becoming *something you do,* and start defining *who you are.* You are not a slave to your passions, but they are a means by which other people may identify with you. Passions open doors of shared interests with others. You will be able to bond with people through your shared passions, and enhance your relationships. You will collect special memories through the passions you both enjoy.

Mastering a passion helps you grow in confidence that will encourage you to strive for even greater achievements. This will be very helpful to you if, like me, you were shy and introverted, and you wish to become more outgoing with others. Passions help you develop your personality and reflect your character.

It is claimed that Abraham Maslow said, *'If all you have is a hammer, everything looks like a nail.'* Take from this the importance of not always talking about the same passion. The more passions you master, the more well-rounded, and the more well-respected you will become. People will take a greater interest in getting to know you.

Recognize that you are a role model, even if you do not think of yourself that way. People will look up to you and perhaps see you as someone they wish to emulate. What will they see when they look at you? What will you show them?

This world is often a difficult place to be, with many temptations and negative activities. The more wholesome, positive diversions you pursue, the more you will enjoy life, and the easier it will be to keep an eternal focus on your salvation. Allow your love of healthy diversions to earn you a spiritual reward that no earthly amusement can equal.

Learn to appreciate the fulfillment that comes from striving for significance. I challenge you to join me in pursuing our passions, and together, we will both continue moving towards mastery.

'Happiness is a by-product of holiness;
it's a benefit of living a pure life, rightly
related to God, self, and others.'
—John Maxwell

To Contact Dave Romeo:

Dave Romeo serves as a personal and professional results coach for people who are dissatisfied with their current results and are serious about doing something to improve them. His greatest areas of expertise are in accomplishing goals, achieving sales success, and developing accountability. Dave also delivers motivational presentations guaranteed to entertain, enlighten, and inspire. For a complete list of all available topics, please go to the seminar menu found at www.DaveRomeo.com.

All of these presentations and services are focused on achieving positive results in the areas of both personal and professional growth and are 100% satisfaction guaranteed. The most current year's general public seminar schedule is also available at www.DaveRomeo.com.

If you wish to obtain a FREE electronic version of the goal list contained in the book *Stumbling Onto Success,* please email Dave Romeo at daveromeo@daveromeo.com.

Dave Romeo also offers a great variety of DVDs, audio CDs, books, and e-books, all of which can be ordered directly from www.DaveRomeo.com.

Please contact Dave Romeo through one of the methods below which offers you the greatest convenience.

Dave Romeo
Dave Romeo Seminars & Coaching
1537 Ridge Road
Elizabethtown, PA 17022
Phone: (717) 413-7472 or (717) 361-2418
E-mail: daveromeo@daveromeo.com
www.daveromeo.com
www.facebook.com/DaveRomeoCoach